The NCTE High School Literature Series

The NCTE High School Literature Series offers classroom teachers in-depth studies of individual writers. Grounded in theory, each volume focuses on a single author and features excerpts from the writer's works, biographical information, and samples of professional literary criticism. Rich in opportunities for classroom discussion and writing assignments that teachers can adapt to their own literature curriculum, each book also offers many examples of student writing.

Volumes in the Series

Nikki Giovanni in the Classroom: "The same ol danger but a brand new pleasure" (1999), Carol Jago

Alice Walker in the Classroom: "Living by the Word" (2000), Carol Jago

Sandra Cisneros in the Classroom: "Do not forget to reach" (2002), Carol Jago

Raymond Carver in the Classroom: "A Small, Good Thing" (2005), Susanne Rubenstein

Amy Tan in the Classroom

"The art of invisible strength"

The NCTE High School Literature Series

Renée H. Shea

Bowie State University, Bowie, Maryland

Deborah L. Wilchek

Rockville High School, Rockville, Maryland

National Council of Teachers of English
1111 W. Kenyon Road, Urbana, Illinois 61801-1096

Cover photo by Robert Foothorap. Reprinted with permission.

Staff Editor: Bonny Graham
Interior Design: Jenny Jensen Greenleaf
Cover Design: Jenny Jensen Greenleaf and Tom Jaczak

NCTE Stock Number: 01488
ISSN 1525-5786

Library of Congress Cataloging-in-Publication Data
Shea, Renée Hausmann.
    Amy Tan in the classroom : "the art of invisible strength" / Renée H. Shea, Deborah L. Wilchek.
        p. cm. — (The NCTE high school literature series)
    Includes bibliographical references.
    ISBN 0-8141-0148-8 (pbk.)
    1. Tan, Amy. Joy Luck Club. 2. Tan, Amy—Study and teaching (Secondary) 3. Tan, Amy—Film and video adaptations. 4. Mothers and daughters in literature. 5. Chinese Americans in literature. I. Wilchek, Deborah L. II. Title. III. Series.
    PS3570.A48J637 2005
    813' .54—dc22

2005013612

To our mothers, Dolores Cunningham and Betty Wainscott, who
give us very visible strength
To Meredith, who brought us together
To Ariel, who "[does her] spiriting gently"

I was six when my mother taught me the art of invisible strength. It was a strategy for winning arguments, respect from others, and eventually, though neither of us knew it at the time, chess games.

—"Rules of the Game," *The Joy Luck Club*

Contents

Permission Acknowledgments.. xi

Acknowledgments... xiii

Introduction.. xv

1. Where Life and Art Intersect...................................... 1

2. Thematic Balance in *The Joy Luck Club*........................... 19

3. Analyzing the Text: Approaches to Close Reading.................. 33

4. Meeting the Challenges of *The Joy Luck Club*.................... 50

5. The Art of Film: *The Joy Luck Club* on Screen.................. 67

6. Taking a Critical Stance: Argument and Assessment..... 90

7. Connections and Extensions...................................... 107

8. More 116

Chronology of Amy Tan's Life...................................... 119

Works Cited... 123

Authors... 127

Permission Acknowledgments

■ ■

Acknowledgments

■ ■

We thank our teacher colleagues for their generosity and wonderful ideas: Sally Lucas, Emily Sigman, Judith Smith, Sean Swanson, Anelle Tumminello, and Julie Zaldumbide. We appreciate the insights and suggestions from our reviewers—Patricia Duncan Bradford, Carol Jago, and Dave Wendelin—and we salute Carol for setting the bar in this series. We thank Clement A. Goddard for his assistance with research and Jennifer Moyers for her help preparing the manuscript.

Most of all, we thank our students past and present.

Introduction

"The art of invisible strength"

When Amy Tan's book of fiction *The Joy Luck Club* came out in 1989, reviewer Carolyn See wrote:

> The only negative thing I could ever say about this book is that I'll never again be able to read it for the first time. *The Joy Luck Club* is so powerful, so full of magic, that by the end of the second paragraph, your heart catches; by the end of the first page, tears blur your vision, and one-third of the way down on page 26, you know you won't be doing anything of importance until you have finished this novel.

We couldn't agree more. We loved *The Joy Luck Club* when we read it for the first time and then again and again; sharing it with our students has only deepened our appreciation of Tan's gift.

When Tan published *The Opposite of Fate: A Book of Musings* in 2003, we noted nonfiction companions to *The Joy Luck Club* on topics that students found compelling. Whether she's writing about her bemused response to seeing the CliffsNotes of *The Joy Luck Club* ("The CliffsNotes Version of My Life"), the film adaptation of her book ("*Joy Luck* and Hollywood"), the joy and pain of speaking a second language ("Mother Tongue"), or even the meaning of books to her eight-year-old self ("What the Library Means to Me"), Tan has a voice that resonates with our students.

And why not? She's played or is playing roles they understand. She was a teenage rebel who resisted the constant family pressure to achieve. The intensity of her relationship with her mother reflects the struggles of many adolescents to define themselves independently of their parents. She tried several careers before settling into one that she felt was an intellectual and spiritual match. A celebrated author who enjoys both commercial success and literary acclaim, Tan still does battle with the written word and depends on her writers' group to support and criticize—to keep her honest. If that's not enough, she's the lead singer for the Rock Bottom Remainders, a rock band that has included fellow writers Barbara Kingsolver, Stephen King, and Dave Barry, performing primarily to raise money for children's literacy programs.

These roles provide context for us to approach *The Joy Luck Club*, Tan's nonfiction, and the film of her book—a "package," if you will, that engages students in thinking about their own "writing tips," telling their own stories, and learning about China and Chinese immigration to the United States at the same time that they see such universals as generational conflicts and the relationship of the past to the present. Students find in Tan a fellow traveler, a searcher. She calls the autobiographical essays in *The Opposite of Fate* a reflection of her search for "a philosophical middle ground between faith and fate" (MacDonald), a search that the students in our classrooms today understand all too well.

In the chapters that follow, we share our own experiences in the classroom, and we are grateful to our colleagues for sharing theirs. Once we began writing about teaching *The Joy Luck Club*, we realized we wanted a larger conversation, to draw on the community of teacher-learners whose ideas tested and deepened our own. We owe a special thanks to teacher-researchers Sally Lucas, Emily Sigman, Judith Smith, Janet Slade Young, and Julie Zaldumbide, whose strategies and ideas tell their stories of meeting the challenges *The Joy Luck Club* can pose in the classroom. We also realized the importance of connecting this discussion to the testing our students face, so we've made suggestions to link *The Joy Luck Club* to the new SAT argument question and the Advanced Placement English exam.

Carolyn See ends her review by describing the lasting impact of Tan's writing:

> *The Joy Luck Club* has the disconcerting effect of making you look at everyone in your own life with the—however fleeting—knowledge that they are locked in the spaceships of their own amazing stories. Only magicians of language like Amy Tan hold the imaginative keys to the isolating capsules. Which is why we have novels and novelists in the first place.

As Tan tells her stories, she helps us—teachers and students alike—find and tell our own. As we explore the pain and triumphs of her characters, we better understand our own struggles. As we listen to her and begin to respond in our own voices, we feel less alone. We've come to understand, as Tan describes in *The Joy Luck Club*, "the art of invisible strength."

1 Where Life and Art Intersect

▪ ▪

When Nick Carraway, the narrator of F. Scott Fitzgerald's classic novel *The Great Gatsby*, points out the impossibility of repeating the past, Jay Gatsby "cries incredulously . . . 'Why of course you can.'" With similar force of will and optimism, Amy Tan's mother argued that her daughter could change the past—as a writer: "She can change it by telling everybody, telling the world" (Davidson 65). That belief in the transformative power of narrative is the unifying thread in Tan's life and a place for students to enter her story and the stories she tells.

A Chinese and American Childhood

Tan was born in Oakland, California, in 1952 and grew up in a bicultural and bilingual household, the only daughter and middle child of John and Daisy Tan. Her father emigrated from China in the late 1940s, just before the Communist Revolution. He had worked for the U.S. Information Service and was trained as an electrical engineer, but when he came to the United States, he became a Baptist minister. Tan's mother had three daughters from an arranged marriage in China, divorced her abusive first husband, and fled to the United States on the last boat to leave Shanghai before the Communist takeover in 1949. After marrying John Tan, she gave birth to her first son, Peter, in 1950 and to John Jr. in 1954.

Tan has spoken about her childhood as characterized by silences about the past. She did not learn of her half sisters until she was an adult, nor about her mother's experiences or those of her grandmother, Jing-mei, the name Tan ultimately chose for the central character of *The Joy Luck Club*. Jing-mei was widowed in the influenza epidemic of 1918 and then raped by a wealthy man who forced her into a life of disgrace as his concubine. She committed suicide in front of her nine-year-old daughter by swallowing raw opium buried in rice cakes. Tan believes that her family history manifests itself in her books as voicelessness and secrets; silence, she says, is "a part of a legacy of . . . the women in my family" (*iVillage*). She describes learning about that history as being "like an excavation—I would find a piece here and there and have to reconfigure it" (*HarperCollins*).

Tan's American name is Amy, her Chinese name An-mei, which means "blessing from America," and this combination characterized her upbringing. In an interview with Elaine Woo for the *Los Angeles Times*, she explains that her parents did not want their children to blend, to assimilate entirely into American culture: "They wanted us to have American circumstances and Chinese character" (14). They had high expectations for their daughter; she was to become a neurosurgeon by career, a concert pianist by avocation. Although as an adult Tan says she recognizes that her parents wanted only the best for her, she remembers the difficulties of trying to live up to their expectations, including nothing less than straight As in school. In her essay "Midlife Confidential," Tan recalls the pressures of her childhood with some humor:

> The word "fun" was not commonly used in our family, except, perhaps, in the following context: "Fun? Why you want have fun? What's so good about this? Just wasting time and money."

In our family, "fun" was a bad ʃ-word, and its antonym was "hard," as in hard work. Things that were hard led to worthwhile results; things that were fun did not.

Another bad ʃ-word was "freedom," as in "So you want American freedom to go wild and bring shame on your family?" Which brings me to another bad ʃ-word, "friends," those purveyors of corruption and shame whose sole purpose in life was to encourage me to talk back to my mother and make her long to return to China, where there were millions of girls my age who would be only too happy to obey their parents without question. The good ʃ-word, of course, was "family," as in "go to church with family," or "do homework with family," or "give your toys to your family in Taiwan." (*Opposite of Fate* 136–37)

During this time, Tan began to show some signs of the writer she would become. When she was in third grade at Matanzas Elementary School, she won a prize for her essay "What the Library Means to Me." In an interview, she says that she simply did what she had learned from her father the minister: "I tried to be very sincere, sort of go for the emotion . . . about how the library is a friend" ("Amy Tan: Best-Selling Novelist"). In this charming piece, reprinted in *The Opposite of Fate*, young Tan had already discovered the persuasive power of metaphor:

I love school because the many things I learn seem to turn on a light in the little room in my mind. I can see a lot of things I have never seen before. . . . My father takes me to the library every two weeks, and I check [out] five or six books each time. These books seem to open many windows in my little room. (269)

Adolescence and College

The struggles and rebellion Tan experienced as a teenager are familiar territory to many of our students, though we hope their lives have not been touched by such tragedy. When she was fifteen, Tan lost both her older brother and her father—within six months—to brain cancer. On the advice of relatives, Daisy moved her remaining family to Europe, first to the Netherlands, then Germany, and eventually Switzerland, where Tan began high school. Her conflicts with her mother escalated, particularly when she began dating a man rumored to be involved with drugs. Tan's mother hired a private detective to investigate her daughter and the wild crowd she had become part of, eventually confirming the boyfriend's illegal activities, as well as uncovering his status as an escaped inmate of a mental institution, and bringing her daughter before a local magistrate. Tan says that her mother's engineering of this confrontation "was the smartest thing she could have done: seeing him no longer had anything to do with rebellion, and I realized I wasn't interested anymore" (Ross, qtd. in Huntley 6).

After Tan graduated from the Institut Monte Rosa in Montreux, Switzerland, the family moved back to the San Francisco area. Her mother chose for her the Baptist Linfield College in Oregon, but after two semesters, Tan decided to transfer to San José City College to be near her Italian American boyfriend, Louis DeMattei, and she changed her major to English—both actions incurring further disapproval from her mother. The two did not speak for over six months. Tan transferred from the City College to San José State University, earned her BA in English and linguistics and an MA in linguistics, and ultimately married DeMattei, now a tax attorney. They have been married for over thirty years.

Tan worked on her doctorate in linguistics at the University of California at Berkeley and had various jobs, including working with children with delayed language development, before she became a freelance business and technical writer. A self-described workaholic, she developed a commercially successful business with prestigious corporate clients such as IBM. In fact, she and her husband earned a sufficient income to buy a house for her mother, a milestone, according to Tan:

> That's really what success is about in Chinese families—it's not success for yourself, it's success so you can take care of your family. And I had achieved that finally; I was able to show her: "I can do well enough to take care of you for the rest of your life; you don't have to worry." (Somogyi and Stanton 27)

In various interviews, Tan has acknowledged her inability to turn down work during this time, leading to ninety-hour work weeks and what she felt was a distorted sense of priorities. She began psychoanalysis, a process she recalls with some humor and which made its way into *The Joy Luck Club* with one of the mothers' disdain about "psyche-atricks." Eventually, she decided to design her own therapy that included taking up jazz piano, an ambitious program of reading fiction, and some attempts at writing. She joined a writers' workshop group in 1985. Essentially, she says, she found meaning in her own life through writing.

Although "Five Writing Tips" was written years later as a commencement address at Simmons College in 2003, the advice Tan offers might have come from this earlier period when she began to understand the relationship between a life of integrity and a writing life. She offers five "tips" that she points out may be "useful in areas other than writing, perhaps even in thinking about life" (*Opposite of Fate* 295). These are

1. Avoid clichés.
2. Avoid generalizations.
3. Find your own voice.

4. Show compassion.

5. Ask the important questions.

"If you hear others using clichés," she writes, "stop to think whether you're being lulled into inaction or the wrong action" (295). Rather than generalities, she suggests paying attention to nuance, advising: "Better to be subtle rather than overbearing, subversive rather than didactic" (296). A person's own voice, she promises, "is one that seeks a personal truth" (296). She warns against the easy temptation of sarcasm, pointing out that "mean-spiritedness is wearying and limited in its one-dimensional point of view" (297). Finally, with a statement that seems to sum up her own fiction and, perhaps, fiction in general, she asserts, "What makes a story worthwhile is the question or questions it poses" (297).

Putting students in the position to offer writing tips is a good way to elicit their own values about writing. It suggests to them, first of all, that they have something to say—tips that a pro might offer the neophyte, the mentor to the apprentice. Second, it asks them to synthesize what they know about writing (or what they've been told) and rank order it. What, exactly, is important? Following is our final exam for an advanced composition course, a creative writing elective, made up of sophomores, juniors, and seniors:

■ ■ ■ ■ ■ ■ ■ ■ ■ ■ ■ ■ ■ ■ ■ ■

Writing Assignment
Read the excerpt from a graduation speech given at Simmons College by the writer Amy Tan. After completing a semester of Advanced Composition, surely you have

your own "five writing tips" to share with others. Clarify
and explain your own tips—those gems and nuggets that
you think are worth passing on to other aspiring writers.
(Reading: Excerpt from Tan's graduation
speech "Five Writing Tips")

Students had more than a notion about the tips that mattered. Since the topic was fairly wide open, some chose to write about essays, others about fiction; different students addressed different parts of the writing process; a few referred to literary works studied in class; some focused on the microlevel of word, others on larger concepts such as audience. Here is a sampling of their responses, excerpts from their longer papers:

> Planning sheets, especially word webs, work wonders. You start off with one word and end up with many new concrete ideas and images that may be jewels to work with since they are so unique. You may be like me and start with "pointe shoes" and finish with "high security."...
>
> It's always hard for a writer to change his or her words, but you MUST edit! Remember to go after stronger verbs and pay attention to diction. Take out unnecessary "to be" and "to get" words, so as never to say "Joe is smarter then Einstein" but "Joe's intelligence surpasses Einstein's."
>
> —*Jueli Li*

> The first and perhaps most important of all is the notion of keeping the subject concrete. Amy Tan rightly mentions this in her own personal list of five, but she assigns it merely second place, and I believe it to have much more importance. Nobody wants to read a story about Existence, History, Life, Sadness, or any other such capitalized form. And even if someone somewhere did desire such a story, it would be impossible to write.

Especially now. Willa Cather may have spoken of the magic age of 15, but at 17, I still do not have the kind of experience to write about Love or Death or Despair, and so forth. It is much more useful to speak of specific situations, to apply general concepts to explicit actions. Instead of an intangible essay about Romance, you have the story of Jay and Daisy or Charles and Emma or Lady Chatterly.

—*Barry Revzin*

Don't be afraid of how people will view your writing. Over the years, one of my main concerns has been if people will understand my writing or not. This has caused me to—instead of making the message of my piece subtle and hidden—bring the main idea right to the surface, screaming it in the faces of my readers until I'm blue with exhaustion. However, I've learned that if I write a clear and well-written paper, my message will come out, no matter how buried it is in my piece.

—*Ira Kowler*

Some students extolled the virtues of expansion, especially the use of detail. Yihan Yang combined form and content in her recommendations: "If I wanted to describe the weather, I can write, *It was windy outside*. A better description could say: *The gust of wind tore at my scarf and nearly pushed me off my feet*."

Others argued for economy. Barry also cautioned against "long-windedness" and used as his support an alternative version of William Carlos Williams's imagistic poem "The Red Wheelbarrow," which he had committed to memory. Imagine, Barry suggests, if the poet had not been succinct, and he offers this revision, acknowledging that it might be a bit "exaggerated":

so much of my life **depends**
upon the events surrounding

a wooden, **red**, decaying **wheel**
barrow with broken wheels

glazed over many times **with rain**
water falling from the heavens

beside, in respect to the farm, **the white**
chickens, dancing happily in the sunrise.

All in all, the students got it! But it's certainly true that once
we teachers ask for advice, we might hear an unexpected voice in
response. Ira also wrote:

> Show, don't tell. This was a no-brainer. As Mrs. Wilchek al-
> ways says, *One of these days, I'm going to get a tattoo on my fore-*
> *head that says, "Show, don't tell."* The only reason Mrs. Wilchek
> would be willing to desecrate her body like that is because the
> mantra of show, don't tell is very important. . . .

Another possibility to engage students in writing about writing or themselves as writers could take off from Tan's rather lengthy
essay "Required Reading and Other Dangerous Subjects." The last
two-and-a-half pages center on her reasons for writing, beginning with "So why do I write?" (*Opposite of Fate* 321). She responds to her own question with a range of creative, humorous,
reflective, and highly metaphorical "answers":

- Because I once thought I couldn't, and I now know I can.
- I write because often I can't express myself any other way, and I
  think I'll implode if I don't find the words.
- I write for very much the same reasons that I read: to startle my
  mind, to churn my heart, to tingle my spine, to knock the blind-
  ers off my eyes and allow me to see beyond the pale.

■ I write because it is the ultimate freedom of expression. And for that reason it is also as scary as skiing down a glacier, as thrilling as singing in a rock-'n'-roll band, as dangerous as falling on your face doing both.

■ Writing to me is an act of faith. (all from *The Opposite of Fate* 322–23)

Though almost anything can be made into an essay assignment, these "why I write" snippets could also be used as a freewrite or warm-up exercise generated by the question "Why do you write?"—although it's probably wise to offer the caveat that no one can respond, "Because my grade depends on it"—or asked as a way to complete a sentence that Tan began (e.g., "I write for very much the same reasons that I read: . . ." Or "I write because I can't . . .").

From Story to Book: *The Joy Luck Club*

Tan claims to have had a lot of luck as she started her career as a novelist. Her first short story, "Endgame," gained her admittance into the Squaw Valley Community of Writers, a fiction writers' workshop. After that story was published in *Seventeen* magazine, the workshop leader sent it to Sandra Dijkstra, a literary agent, who became interested in Tan and encouraged her to write a full novel. "Endgame" centered on a chess prodigy, prefiguring the section in *The Joy Luck Club* on Waverly Jong.

Life and art did indeed intersect for Tan when, in 1986, her mother suffered a heart attack. The urgency of learning more about her mother, of truly getting to know her, increased, along with Tan's interest in her Chinese heritage. She made her first trip to China in 1987 with her mother and husband and met her half sisters. Tan says that this trip was a life-changing experience that gave her a sense of completeness: "I felt in some way that I belonged, that I had found a country related to me (Pearlman and Henderson, qtd. in Huntley 10).

The time was apparently right. Tan returned to San Francisco to find that Dijkstra had negotiated a $50,000 advance for her—yet unwritten—book. Tan finished it in four months, claiming she feared that what she viewed as an extraordinary opportunity would be taken away. The book, originally titled *Wind and Water*, was renamed *The Joy Luck Club*, and the rest has become literary legend. In this narrative about mothers and daughters, Tan began telling the stories of intergenerational and cultural conflicts, the search for identity, and the desire to break silence that would continue into three more novels and two children's books. Although she denies any one-to-one autobiographical correlations between one of the daughters and mothers in the book and herself and her mother, she writes in "Mother Tongue": "the reader I decided on was my mother, because these were stories about mothers" (*Opposite of Fate* 278).

The Joy Luck Club was an immediate success, with generally favorable reviews, more than nine months on the *New York Times* bestseller list, sales exceeding four million copies, nominations for the National Book Award and the National Book Critics Circle Award, and a $1.23 million sale for the paperback rights. It has been translated into more than twenty languages, including Chinese. In 1989, *The Joy Luck Club* became a major motion picture.

Stories seem a perfect entranceway into *The Joy Luck Club* for students. Since this book has a tricky narrative made up of four interlocking sections (each with an opening fable and four vignettes), just being able to identify and follow specific story lines is essential to an appreciation of the work. Furthermore, *The Joy Luck Club* explores what we know, how we know it, the role of memory in personal history, and the importance of viewpoint in understanding our experience. An assignment that students find accessible yet revealing is to write their own stories in response to a quotation from *The Joy Luck Club*.

■ ■ ■ ■ ■ ■ ■ ■ ■ ■ ■ ■ ■ ■ ■ ■ ■

Writing Assignment

Use the following quotation as a starting point and "flesh out" one of the stories begun in the following quotation. Spend approximately 15 minutes on this task. (Your story does not need to be any specific length; if you don't finish in 15 minutes, you are welcome to write "to be continued," but do make every effort to bring the story to a close within that time frame.) Remember, I am not expecting a polished piece—nor will you receive a grade. This is an opportunity to explore!

"Oh, what good stories! Stories spilling out all over the place! We almost laughed to death. A rooster that ran into the house screeching on top of dinner bowls, the same bowls that held him quietly in pieces the next day! And one about a girl who wrote love letters for two friends who loved the same man. And a silly foreign lady who fainted on a toilet when firecrackers went off next to her." (*The Joy Luck Club* 24)

■ ■ ■ ■ ■ ■ ■ ■ ■ ■ ■ ■ ■ ■ ■ ■ ■

Students chose different perspectives, focusing on love letters, firecrackers, or the rooster. The writing that resulted from this assignment with a class of sophomores, juniors, and seniors averaged one to two pages, and it had the raw emotion and action characteristic of first drafts. Perhaps most important, students had fun.

Tuquynh Le got right into the action with "Rooroo and His Harem":

> I begin scattering the crumbs, this way and that, me, the ultimate crouton sprinkler system. The chickens behave relatively well, pecking my shoes to get at more but nothing worse. And then I come to Roo's domain. He's strutting towards me now, beak clicking, feet stomping, feathers fluffed and ready to go. Ah . . . sprinkle and scatter, sprinkle and scatter. . . .
> Soul searing, burning, pinching, pain, and a splatter of red. Rooroo pulls back, eyes flashing proud with his tie dyed beak cocked to the side. I will have my revenge, Roo, you just wait! The side of my hands bleeds profusely, leaving a trail of red as I walk back into the house. I may have lost a battle to a rooster, but I have my pride!
>
> —*Tuquynh Le*

Clearly a plot girl, Tuquynh has the action verbs, cinematic images, and escalating conflict that launch a writer into a story. The pose of the narrator speaking to the rooster adds humor even as it suggests an impending shoot-out, antagonists about to do battle.

One of the challenges for us as teachers is to help students understand what their choices are. When a question asks for "elements of style" or students need to "write an essay," what are the choices available to them? What's the repertoire? In this assignment, narrative stance, although not specified as an issue or focus, is central as students make quick decisions about who is telling the story. Joanne decided to write as the rooster's predator—to write in his diary, no less. Here are two excerpts:

Dear Diary:

    The people at the farm got a guard rooster today. Weasel told me. He was walking down the deer path with a big smirk on his face, kind of like the one he had the time Mrs. Woolf's favorite cub got taken into that pack from across the mountain, and he got to tell her the news. . . . Anyhoo, the rooster is supposed to stay up all night when the chickens are asleep to warn the people when I come. I didn't realize I was that special.

Dear Diary:
Hungry. Miserable, cold, wet. Slimy. It rained this morning and part of the den caved in. Should get back to work.
                                               —*Joanne Buchbinder*

Joanne indicated that she was deciding to change perspectives as she wrote, but the very idea of becoming the rooster (which she does in the second entry) is delightful. And, of course, changing your mind is part and parcel of any first draft.

    Other students inclined toward character studies. Again, the visual prevails in the following description by Angela Jiang, who was inspired by the foreign lady on the toilet. She offers a double narrative frame (i.e., the speaker identifies her brother as the storyteller), describes the physical details of the lady's appearance, and then sets the stage for a conflict to be explored. Following is the opening paragraph of three:

My brother retold the story, choking on his dumplings, hands flying everywhere in frantic gestures. The whole town had turned out to meet her; she was the granddaughter of one of the village elders, but had lived in the States her entire life. A joke from the start: she wore a tight skirt that picked up dust and dirt as soon as she stepped off the cab. Thin fingers clutched her leather purse, afraid of some unknown disease. Xiao Hao, the village cherub, ran up and offered her some lee-chees as a welcoming gift, but—oh, what nerve!—she gasped and stumbled back muttering about larvae. Outsider, some called her; idiot, others muttered. The bad feeling crept up inside us, a mixture of guilt and annoyance. How dare she act like she was above us? She wouldn't sleep on the ground, she wouldn't walk on the dirt paths barefoot, she wouldn't kowtow at the family temples.

—*Angela Jiang*

As students discover their own storytelling voices and potential, we like to alert them to the stories all around them—in their families, friends, and communities—and encourage them to become aware of different ways to tell those stories. Again, Tan herself is instructive, as she recalls the distinct styles of her parents:

In an interview with Gretchen Giles, Amy Tan reveals that she learned the craft of story construction from her father, a very busy Baptist minister who managed to spend quality time with his children by reading his sermons to them and then asking for their opinions on content and language. Tan recalls that her father's sermons were written in narrative form, as carefully crafted stories. She also points out that in contrast to her father's carefully designed narratives, most of her mother's stories were neither formally constructed nor refined but rather evolved out of the daily life, activities, and conversations of the extended family. Daisy Tan, a talented natural storyteller, exchanged family news and stories of local events with other women . . . as they sat preparing vegetables or other ingredients for cooking. (Huntley 15)

The Writing Life

Since the success of *The Joy Luck Club*, Amy Tan has written three novels and two children's books. In "Angst and the Second Novel," in *The Opposite of Fate*, she described the pressure of trying to follow such unusual success and, in fact, the difficulty of writing when she had so many requests for speaking engagements. But she need not have worried: *The Kitchen God's Wife* (1991) received critical praise, with reviewers applauding the mature writer. Tan says that her mother tired of being asked if she was the model for the mothers (or one of them) in *The Joy Luck Club* and suggested that she actually tell Daisy's story in her second novel. *The Hundred Secret Senses* (1995), a magical realist novel about the conflicts between two half sisters, also became an international bestseller.

Her mother was diagnosed with Alzheimer's disease in 1995, the year Amy Tan began writing her fourth novel. "I wanted to write a story about memory," she says, "but in a way I suppose I thought that I would keep her alive—as long as I had to write this book, she would need to stay around" (*HarperCollins*). After her mother died in 1999, Tan completed *The Bonesetter's Daughter* (2001), which explores the bonds of mothers and daughters through another series of interlocking stories, this time centering on a contemporary woman, her mother, and the past that links them.

Tan has also written two children's books, *The Moon Lady* (1992) and *Sagwa, the Chinese Siamese Cat* (1994). In 2003 she published *The Opposite of Fate*, what she calls "a book of musings" about the mysteries of fate and faith. The pieces in this collection run the gamut, from her essay on the library, to her lighthearted response to seeing the CliffsNotes of *The Joy Luck Club*, to her poignant reflection on the deaths of her father and brother and the murder of a dear college friend, whose ghost she believes lived on for a while in her computer. In the title essay, she recounts how she is currently coping with the effects of Lyme disease and the long, painful process that led to her diagnosis and recovery.

Ethnicity and Universality

Although Tan has influenced an entire generation of readers and writers and acknowledges that she is a role model for many, especially Chinese Americans, she refuses what she calls "the burden" of representing a particular culture and warns against "balkanizing literature" ("The Spirit Within"). Rather than seeing herself as writing about "cultural dichotomies," she says she is writing about "human connections" ("The Spirit Within"). She has, she asserts, her story to tell, perhaps her stories, but not *the* story of any entire group. Thus, she does not believe that she appeals more to an audience of one ethnicity or background than another. Her work, she hopes, contributes to her view of what fiction can do for all of us: "reading good fiction can help enrich what you notice in life[;] . . . it is like a meditation on what details you might also observe and bring into your own life. Reading helps you live well and fully" (Edwards).

One way to emphasize to our students the "human connections" in Tan's work, particularly in *The Joy Luck Club*, is to make comparisons with other works about parents and children, and poetry is a good place to start. Poems on the bonds between mothers and daughters include "The Pomegranate" by Eavan Boland and "The Bistro Styx" by Rita Dove (both based on the Persephone-Demeter myth). Others include "Little Girl, My Stringbean" by Anne Sexton and "To a Daughter Leaving Home" by Linda Pastan. "Mother to Son" by Langston Hughes explores the relationship the title names, and in "The Writer" by Richard Wilbur a father reflects on his daughter and her writing life. W. B. Yeats's "A Prayer for My Daughter" is another classic. Father-son poems include "Those Winter Sundays" by Robert Hayden, "My Papa's Waltz" by Theodore Roethke, and "A Story" and "The Gift" by Li-Young Lee. Any of these lays a smooth foundation for studying *The Joy Luck Club* and reminds students of generational conflicts and bonds that cross all other boundaries—regardless of gender, age, ethnicity, and cultural experiences. We think Amy Tan would like the company.

■ ■ ■ ■ ■ ■ ■ ■ ■ ■ ■ ■ ■ ■ ■ ■ ■

Reading Assignment

Read Tan's opening essay "The CliffsNotes Version of My Life" in *The Opposite of Fate* to get a taste of her life from her viewpoint—and of her humor. She explains the origin of the phrase "invisible strength" with amusing scatological references, for instance, and tells the apocalyptic story of her mother determining to move the family to Holland [the Netherlands] because it was "a clean place" after seeing a picture on the Dutch Cleanser can. Many of her insights are told lightheartedly yet carry a powerful punch; for example, she recalls the perceptual transformation from her American teenage self as "dateless dork" to "*exotique*" when she moved to Europe. (30)

■ ■ ■ ■ ■ ■ ■ ■ ■ ■ ■ ■ ■ ■ ■ ■ ■

2 Thematic Balance in *The Joy Luck Club*

■ ■

"To me, that's what the stories are about: the search for balance in my life," says Amy Tan in her revealing essay "Required Reading and Other Dangerous Subjects" (*Opposite of Fate* 302). No wonder the word *balance* appears so frequently in *The Joy Luck Club*. In the opening vignette, Jing-mei notes as she takes her mother's place at the mahjong table that "[s]omething was not in balance" (31). Later, in "Half and Half," Rose Hsu Jordan comments on her mother's faith as a "way for her [mother] to correct the imbalances of life" (116). In "Rice Husband," Lena recalls the beginning moments of her relationship with her husband Harold as a time when she was "caught off balance" (155).

Tan herself explains the book's structure by pointing out that "there are really only three narrators who are mothers, not four, as some reviewers and students have noted" (*Opposite of Fate* 302). Having the three mothers at the mahjong table was a deliberate decision, she says, "to create a sense of imbalance, a feeling that something or someone was missing" (302). To her, the stories are really about this "search for balance" (302). Taking our cue from the author, we've had the most success in the classroom by exploring *The Joy Luck Club* through several themes, all framed as tensions that resist balance and harmony.

Pacing the Reading

Before we discuss specific themes, however, we want to say a word about reading the entire book. With increasing and alarming frequency, some students graduate from high school claiming that they've seldom read an entire book. They've read excerpts, stories, and essays but few whole books. One of the reasons *The Joy Luck Club* is such a teachable text is that it matches the reading styles of many students and is ideally suited to a reading "installment plan." Structurally, *The Joy Luck Club* has sixteen interlocking narratives divided into four sections, each with four stories and prefaced with a short fable. The individual sections—each between sixty and seventy pages—are natural breaking points for reading assignments and discussion.

Tan says that she used the fables in organizing her book to create a structure that is "an emotional one, linked by a small fable . . . that resonated for each piece" (*Opposite of Fate* 304). Before assigning the book as independent reading, we like to start with all four of the fables, treating them as a continuous narrative. We read them aloud in class and unpack the emotional structure in each. This strategy enables students to make connections and predict themes that Tan will develop. Then they start reading the quartet of stories with the initial fable as a unifying lens. Table 2.1 identifies the fable, a central question relating to theme, and the quartet of stories.

After students have read one quartet of stories, we ask, "What do these four stories have in common?" Through a series of activities and discussions based on the questions in this table, four themes begin to emerge, each focused on contraries in need of balance: good intentions and bad luck, obedience and rebellion, loss and gain, and ignorance and knowledge. The activity-based assignments we discuss in this chapter engage students in con-

Table 2.1

Fable	Question	Stories
"Feathers from a Thousand Li Away" (the story of the mother's gift to her daughter of the swan feather, of her good intentions)	How do the four stories illustrate a mother's good intentions/bad luck?	"The Joy Luck Club" "Scar" "The Red Candle" "The Moon Lady"
"The Twenty-Six Malignant Gates" (the story of the rebellious daughter's reactions to her mother's demands)	How do the four stories illustrate a daughter's rebellion against/obedience to her mother?	"Rules of the Game" "The Voice from the Wall" "Half and Half" "Two Kinds"
"American Translation" (the story of a mother's warnings— superstitions—about loss and the daughter's reaction to that warning)	How do the four stories illustrate a mother's warning or advice to her daughter about loss/ discovery?	"Rice Husband" "Four Directions" "Without Wood" "Best Quality"
"Queen Mother of the Western Skies" (a conversation between a woman and her infant granddaughter and the woman's efforts to teach her daughter [the baby's mother] "how to lose [her] innocence but not [her] hope. How to laugh forever.")	How do these four stories illustrate the idea of moving from ignorance to knowl- edge?	"Magpies" "Waiting between the Trees" "Double Face" "A Pair of Tickets"

structing meaning—that is, in moving from often disparate story lines, settings, and characters to unifying ideas and themes. Following is our introduction to these four themes and the activities we use for discussion and assessment in lieu of more traditional study guide questions.

Theme 1: Good Intentions and Bad Luck

One theme in *The Joy Luck Club* concerns the hopes of a character for the "good" life that are offset by "bad" decisions or events. In this first section, titled "Feathers from a Thousand Li Away," the mother tells her daughter, "This feather may look worthless, but it comes from afar and carries with it all my good intentions" (17). Suyuan in "The Joy Luck Club" escapes from the Japanese invasion of Kweilin but not before she must leave "everything" (26) behind, a decision that haunts her for the rest of her life. An-mei, in "Scar," remembers her mother's return after her bad luck of being disowned by family. Since her grandmother is ill, the well-intentioned mother honors her by cutting off a piece of her own flesh and making a healing soup. Lindo, in "The Red Candle," recalls her arranged marriage and escape from it by exploiting her in-laws' superstitious beliefs. In "The Moon Lady," Ying-ying recalls her privileged childhood and her bad luck at the Moon Festival when she fell overboard.

Theme 2: Obedience and Rebellion

The tension between an individual's desire to assert herself and the obligation to honor and respect her parents is a theme that unifies the second group of stories. Indeed, the word *gate* in the title of the fable suggests the tension between the obedience of staying within expectations and rules and the rebellion that exit brings. As Waverly, Jing-mei, Lena, and Rose negotiate their Ameri-

can environment that prizes individuality, they struggle to distinguish themselves from their parents' values and expectations in
ways most teenagers that we teach understand very well. The
mothers' stories also remind our students that parents were once
young and often experienced the same struggles their children
may repeat.

In "Rules of the Games," Waverly recalls her success as a child
chess prodigy and her embarrassment at her mother's bragging.
Briefly running away from home, Waverly rebels and refuses to
play chess again. In "The Voice from the Wall," Lena St. Clair
chronicles her mother's loss of a baby and subsequent mental
breakdown. Lena compares her own silent rebellion with her
neighbor's more vocal one. In "Half and Half," as Rose faces divorce, she finds herself in conflict with her mother, who opposes
her divorce, and suddenly the tables are turned: Rose did not
obey her mother, who opposed the marriage to a non-Asian man,
and now she finds herself rebelling against her mother's belief
that dissolving that marriage in divorce is wrong. A frequently
anthologized story, "Two Kinds" chronicles the tension between
June and her mother as Suyuan attempts to make her daughter
into a piano prodigy. After a disastrous and humiliating piano
recital, June rebels and refuses to play piano again.

Theme 3: Loss and Gain

In examining this thematic idea, we ask students to consider the
four stories in "American Translation" as a tension between the
loss of something such as a place, a loved one, or a belief and the
gain of finding another place, a greater understanding, a different
sense of self. Does each of the daughters and mothers experience
some kind of psychological or emotional loss but eventually "find
herself"? Lena's reflections in "Rice Husband," for example, con-

trast the stark beauty of her expensive home and her seeming success in her husband's architecture firm with the lost joys of their early relationship and her growing realization that their marriage is "just not enough" (160). "Best Quality" reveals June's memories of a dinner before her mother's death, when June was insulted and embarrassed by Waverly's comments about her work. As June discusses with her mother her sense of lost identity, her mother comforts her with a jade pendant, her "life's importance" (197), a gift suggesting a found heritage. In "Four Directions," Waverly revisits her childhood chess experience and the loss of her skill. As she worries about her mother's approval of Rich, her new American boyfriend, she comes to the realization that her mother is really just "an old woman" (183), and for a moment she is able to break down the barriers between them. Although Rose, in "Without Wood," has acquiesced to all of her husband Ted's demands about their divorce and the impending sale of their house, she begins to recognize that she really has found herself and understands what she wants. As her mother suggests, she can speak up for herself.

Theme 4: Ignorance and Knowledge

Each of the central characters in the fourth quartet of stories embarks on a journey that reveals her growing awareness and understanding of family. In "Waiting between the Trees," an older Ying-ying recalls her difficult first marriage, the loss of her young son, her remarriage, and her efforts to find her spirit again and pass it on to her daughter. An-mei in "Magpies" describes her life in Wu Tsing's house, where her mother is his lowly fourth wife. She remembers with great sorrow her mother's unhappiness and subsequent suicide, yet through this painful knowledge An-mei finds herself and "learn[s] to shout" (240). The story of Waverly and Lindo, her mother, continues in "Double Face." As they wait together at the beauty parlor, Lindo and Waverly confront their past tensions and come to realize their physical and emotional similarities. The final story of the book, "A Pair of Tickets," reveals June's journey to China to connect with her half sisters, a connection that leads her to understand how much they and she are the spirit of their mother.

Constructing Meaning: Four Activities

We want students to "dance" with this book and feel the same life in the stories and characters that we feel. We rarely assign lists of study questions, though we occasionally pose a focus question or ask them to construct one. But we prefer a repertoire of activities that engages students with the text on several levels: the most literal one of tracing events and making sense of them, another involving interpreting passages of text, and others that take them inside the book's characters and structure. Following are four possibilities.

The most direct activity is a graphic organizer or **balance sheet** to guide students as they read and discuss. Our intent here is to help students focus on a central character in a story, but then, to avoid a "CliffsNotes" response, we also include a requirement for textual analysis and inference that could lead to a more thematic reading. We try to represent visually the idea of balance (see Figure 2.1).

Once students have captured their ideas and impressions for one of the stories (or more than one), they have significant observations to contribute to class discussion. We divide into groups for discussion. Each group gets a blank overhead transparency of the graphic organizer, and the group members share their individual responses. They then work until they reach consensus, fill

---

A Balance Sheet

As you read the stories, complete this graphic organizer. Bring it to class so you can participate in the discussion.

Good Intentions (examples of)	Important Quotation and Explanation

Central Character's Name	
Key Character Traits (evidence of)	Bad Luck (examples of)

Figure 2.1

in the graphic organizer on the transparency, and report to the entire class.

Another way we encourage active reading and critical thinking is to use **dialectical journals**. This activity is beneficial, especially for younger (ninth or tenth grade) or less experienced readers, because it anchors them in the language of the book. Figure 2.2 provides an example of a basic type of dialectical journal in which students begin to develop their own interpretations by responding to specific quotations. Note that they choose their own quotations.

Dialectical Journal on *The Joy Luck Club*
For each story or vignette, in the left-hand column write down four or five quotations that you think are significant, powerful, interesting, thought provoking, or puzzling. In the right-hand column, react to and explain the quotes you selected.

Story Title: "Waiting between the Trees"

What the Story Says	What I Think
Her wisdom is like a bottomless pond. You throw stones in and they sink into the darkness and dissolve. Her eyes looking back do not reflect anything. *I think this to myself even though I love my daughter. She and I have shared the same body. There is a part of her mind that is part of mine. But when she was born, she sprang from me like a slippery fish, and has been swimming away ever since. (242)*	*Water, fish—images of start of life. Sinking stones and darkness vs. being saved. Mother is worried. But why is daughter's wisdom like a bottomless pond—sounds.*
She does not know how beautiful I was when I married this man. I was far more pretty than my daughter, who has country feet and a large nose like her father's. *Even today, my skin is still smooth, my figure like a girl's. But there are deep lines in my mouth where I used to wear smiles. . . . (246)*	*Mother feels distance—she's sad and angry at daughter's lack of awareness. Maybe she's jealous. She claims to feel superior (she was prettier), but she seems to be unsure of herself.*
It is because I had so much joy then that I came to have so much hate. (247)	*Opposites are close—maybe like mothers and daughters.*
When my daughter looks at me, she sees a small old lady. That is	*Distance again—daughter does not appreciate mother for what she once*

continued on next page

Figure 2.2

because she sees only with her outside eyes. She has no chuming, *no inside knowing of things. If she had* chuming, *she would see a tiger lady. And she would have careful fear. (248)*	*was. What if the mother actually said these things to her daughter? Does she want her daughter to be afraid of her?*
Now I must tell my daughter everything. That she is the daughter of a ghost. She has no chi. *This is my greatest shame. How can I leave this world without leaving her my spirit? (252)*	*Will she tell her? I doubt it. The mother doesn't have enough spirit left to give to her daughter.*

Figure 2.2 continued

These dialectical journals are another way to reinforce balance as a central motif through a visual representation. In addition, as they mine the text, students feel empowered because they are selecting their own quotes and making their own meaning. A variation on this dialectical journal is to have one student list quotes that interest him or her and then exchange journals with another student, who fills in the reaction column.

Both the balance sheet and the dialectical journal work well to help students explore theme, but we like to mix these types of activities with less text-based activities, such as transformational assignments. Through these activities, we hope to guide students toward a deeper understanding of the central characters and their relationships with one another and to reflect on the theme(s) being revealed in the stories. Basically, we ask our students to transform prose pieces into **dramatic scripts** and present them to their classmates (see Figure 2.3).

As students get involved in this activity (which is likely to take up several class periods), they truly study the characters and

---

A Dramatic Transformation

1. Use one of the assigned stories (such as "Scar," "The Red Candle," "Two Kinds," "Rules of the Game," etc.)

2. Work in small groups on one story. Write a dramatic script (a collaborative effort) that captures a central theme. You may need to condense the story, but stay true to the characters and their relationships with one another. You can add a narrator if you need to, but be sure to include enough characters to keep the entire group involved. Remember that your central characters will need to consider the following questions: Who am I? How am I supposed to act? What do I want?

3. After completing your script, get your acting troupe ready. Prepare to present your dramatic scene to your classmates. Plan and practice entrances, exits, and positions. Think about how characters will deliver their lines and how the relationships among them will be revealed. Add any props or costumes that you think will bring the drama to life. Your presentation should be ten to fifteen minutes long.

4. After staging your production, be prepared to answer any questions the audience may have about your dramatic rendering, the theme, or the story itself.

Figure 2.3

their actions from the inside out. The liveliness of the productions is exciting and energizing for both actors and audience, though the extent to which students enter into the production aspect (with costumes and props) varies, often depending on their age. Usually, the discussions about decisions of what to include or exclude in the scripts show insight and understanding of the characters that might not come up in the regular classroom discussions. Most important, the question-and-answer sessions after the presentations encourage all students to think about the stories, the characters, and the themes.

The epiphanies that each character in *The Joy Luck Club* undergoes are significant, arguably the essence of the book. So, to give our students opportunities to "experience" these epiphanies in some form that brings them closer than simply reading about the character, we chose an **ecphrastic response**, a term used in the art world to describe the tradition of responding, through a variety of stances, to a work of art (think Keats and "Ode on a Grecian Urn"). An ecphrastic response requires the creator to enter completely into the spirit and essence of the work. While much ecphrastic writing is poetic in nature, we expanded the possibilities to encourage students to experiment with different genres (see Figure 2.4).

In the spirit of that final admonition to share, it seemed right for the teacher to try her hand. Here's one that Debbie wrote as a model in which the voice of Lindo remembers her husband's proposal and reveals her hopes and dreams for her daughter Waverly:

An Ecphrastic Response

Create an ecphrastic response to one of the stories in *The Joy Luck Club*. Select any of the modes of expression below—but remember to get to the essence of the character's journey and to reveal the theme in your creation.

Suggested modes: a poem, a recipe, an advertisement, a diary entry, an advice column, an interview, a song, a comic strip or cartoon, an e-mail message, a collage, a news broadcast, a commentary by a minor character.

Be prepared to share with the rest of the class!

Figure 2.4

Lindo's Poem (based on "Double Face")

"Lindo, can you spouse me?"
I watch the words
Tumble out of his mouth
My name first —
The tip of his tongue
Knocking against the back of his teeth
Like Mah jong tiles on the table
And then this funny word
"spouse."
A rhyme with house
Like in the fortune cookie
I gave him on purpose
(my good intention)
But the way he says this word
Travels long and hangs in the air
Between us
Even though my English
Is not much better,
I know the word is wrong
And I laugh at him,
Hiding my smiling teeth
Behind my hand
But by the end of the day
We agree to spouse.
And before long there are Winston and Vincent
And the last one
Who looks so much like me
And I want the best for her
Best circumstance
Best character
And I want her to belong here
To this place,
This new country of mine
With the long hills and
The strange ways.

So she becomes Waverly
The name of the street we live on
And she belongs.

On to the Essay . . .

While Table 2.1 illustrates a neat correlation of story to theme, clearly the themes we've examined run throughout the book and are not limited to any particular section. In fact, students begin to notice on their own that a theme discussed in one quartet of stories continues to develop in another set. But, then, isn't that really what a theme does? As they begin to see how a writer weaves and interweaves ideas throughout a novel, students are learning how fiction works. *The Joy Luck Club* gives us a wonderful opportunity to teach this all-important lesson.

■ ■ ■ ■ ■ ■ ■ ■ ■ ■ ■ ■ ■ ■ ■ ■

Writing Assignment
Write an essay on *The Joy Luck Club* analyzing one of the four thematic tensions we have focused on in class—good intentions and bad luck, obedience and rebellion, lost and found, and ignorance and knowledge. Explain the nature of the tension and consider whether it is resolved. If it is, how is it? If it is not, what forces prevent a resolution?

■ ■ ■ ■ ■ ■ ■ ■ ■ ■ ■ ■ ■ ■ ■ ■

3 Analyzing the Text: Approaches to Close Reading

■ ■

Reading at Risk, the 2004 National Endowment for the Arts report stating that reading is on the decline (www.nea.gov/pub/ReadingAtRisk.pdf), came as no surprise to those of us who are in today's classrooms, nor is it likely to stop us from continuing to teach—and preach—the joys of the written word. Not only do most of us who count ourselves English teachers love to read, but we also love to talk about what we read, analyze it, and burrow into the writer's craft. On the one hand, we want our students to share our fascination with how language creates meaning, for the sheer joy of appreciating the artistry. On the other hand, with increasing frequency, students are facing the practical reality of being required to analyze how language creates meaning on standardized tests, including district and state assessments and Advanced Placement and International Baccalaureate exams.

Close reading may not come naturally but responding to language does. In our classrooms, we've tried out many approaches to analyzing written text, and we agree that the key is having a rich and layered text to start with. *The Joy Luck Club* fits that bill. We can open up *The Joy Luck Club* at nearly any spot and find a passage that works on its own or in context to show a gifted writer at work. Another lesson our students have taught us is that no one approach is best; we need a range of ways for them to conceptualize the effect of the choices a writer makes.

What we offer in this chapter are three possibilities for approaching close reading at different junctures in the reading process: first, as a way to introduce a longer work; second, as a means to keep track of character traits and lay the groundwork for studying character development; and third, as a way to do a close textual reading of a passage within a work the students are studying.

Interrupted Reading as Introduction to Text

One way to introduce a longer piece—a novel, a play, even a substantial short story—is to give students information about the author, the time period, background to the work, perhaps a preview of plot, a glimpse into the characters. . . . And while this can work, it can also be pretty dull. What we find ourselves asking is, "What do students really need to know or have in mind as they start a longer work?" The fairly obvious answer seems to be: as much of the writer's world as possible, questions that the longer text might answer, enough interest to read on. We call our strategy an "interrupted reading": we isolate a passage to enable students to experience the text bit by bit. This approach discourages their inclination to search for "the meaning" and encourages them to jump into what's right in front of them.

Very often a good choice for an interrupted reading is the opening passage from a novel. The opening to *Heart of Darkness* by Joseph Conrad or to *Song of Solomon* by Toni Morrison, for instance, contains just about every theme in the novel and thus works well to introduce it. But in *The Joy Luck Club*, we choose a passage nearer the end, from "Double Face," the scene in the beauty parlor where Lindo Jong is having her hair done for her daughter's wedding. This section contains many of the concerns and themes of the entire book (e.g., mother-daughter conflicts, intersection of past and present), and it's a study in "seeing" and "reflecting." Here are a few steps for developing an interrupted reading:

■ Find a passage that is long enough to divide into several sections but not so long that the process becomes tedious. Four or five sections seems about right.

■ Type up one section of the passage per page so that students will read these individually. (If photocopying is a problem, use an overhead projector or the computer screen.)

■ Remind students that they will move through the process as a whole group. That is, someone will read one passage out loud, then everyone will write, then someone will read the next passage, everyone will write, and so on. We tell them that if they read a passage and feel they've said everything they have to say, reread it. Treat it like music: "listen" to it again.

■ Invite students to respond to each section of the passage in any way at all. They might free-associate with something they read, question it, or argue against it. They might note a technique or a figure of speech. They should feel free to write phrases or sentences, underline or draw connecting lines, or comment anywhere at all. They can register confusion or even dislike. But it's important to write something down.

■ Reserve discussion until the end. This gives students a chance to go through the entire passage following one train of thought or developing an idea (or disproving one) without hearing a classmate's response.

■ Use a different reader for each passage because one reader (especially the teacher) might convey an interpretation, even unintentionally, through voice inflection and tone.

We divide this passage from *The Joy Luck Club* into five sections. We wanted the first of these sections to be a short piece that would accustom students to the voices in the passage and set up the conflict. In terms of technique, it includes both description and dialogue as well as a hint of the irony that will dominate the passage. In the second, longer section, we wanted all three voices, again with the mother's thoughts dominating. The communication or lack of it between mother and daughter is heightened here, and the visual image of the mother looking at herself in the mirror and talking to the image of her daughter that she sees in that mirror is striking. The third section is a short paragraph that introduces the cultural dislocation "my American face . . . the face Americans think is Chinese" (255) and the conflict between shame and pride that is at the heart of the book. Almost as though it's a plot in and of itself, the fourth section heats up, with the hairdresser unwittingly making a comment that brings the simmering mother-daughter conflict to a boil. The brief final section belongs to the mother, who not only has the last word but also introduces another generation. The passage, essentially, comes full circle.

Interrupted Reading Passage from *The Joy Luck Club*

1.

My daughter is getting married a second time. So she asked me to go to her beauty parlor, her famous Mr. Rory. I know her meaning. She is ashamed of my looks. What will her husband's parents and his important lawyer friends think of this backward old Chinese woman?

"Auntie An-mei can cut me," I say.

"Rory is famous," says my daughter, as if she had no ears. "He does fabulous work."

2.

So I sit in Mr. Rory's chair. He pumps me up and down until I am the right height. Then my daughter criticizes me as if I were not there. "See how it's flat on one side," she accuses my head. "She needs a cut and a perm. And this purple tint in her hair, she's been doing it at home. She's never had anything professionally done."

She is looking at Mr. Rory in the mirror. He is looking at me in the mirror. I have seen this professional look before. Americans don't really look at one another when talking. They talk to their reflections. They look at others or themselves only when they think nobody is watching. So they never see how they really look. They see themselves smiling without their mouths open, or turned to the side where they cannot see their faults.

"How does she want it?" asked Mr. Rory. He thinks I do not understand English. He is floating his fingers through my hair. He is showing how his magic can make my hair thicker and longer.

"Ma, how do you want it?" Why does my daughter think she is translating English for me? Before I can even speak, she explains my thoughts: "She wants a soft wave. We probably shouldn't cut it too short. Otherwise it'll be too tight for the wedding. She doesn't want it to look kinky or weird."

And now she says to me in a loud voice, as if I had lost my hearing, "Isn't that right, Ma? Not too tight?"

3.

I smile. I use my American face. That's the face Americans think is Chinese, the one they cannot understand. But inside I am becoming ashamed. I am ashamed she is ashamed. Because she is my daughter and I am proud of her, and I am her mother but she is not proud of me.

4.

Mr. Rory pats my hair more. He looks at me. He looks at my daughter. Then he says something to my daughter that really displeases her: "It's uncanny how much you two look alike!"

I smile, this time with my Chinese face. But my daughter's eyes and her smile become very narrow, the way a cat pulls itself small just before it bites. Now Mr. Rory goes away so we can think about this. I hear him snap his fingers, "Wash! Mrs. Jong is next!"

So my daughter and I are alone in this crowded beauty parlor. She is frowning at herself in the mirror. She sees me looking at her.

"The same cheeks," she says. She points to mine and then pokes her cheeks. She sucks them outside in to look like a starved person. She puts her face next to mine, side by side, and we look at each other in the mirror.

"You can see your character in your face," I say to my daughter without thinking. "You can see your future."

"What do you mean?" she says.

5.
And now I have to fight back my feelings. These two faces, I think, so much the same! The same happiness, the same sadness, the same good fortune, the same faults.

I am seeing myself and my mother, back in China, when I was a young girl.

(254–56)

Most, though not all, students respond well to such an interrupted reading. They enjoy the fact that they truly can make any comment—nothing's "wrong"—and that they can roll around in the language. In many cases, they worry about plot, fretting about what's going on as they begin, but a well-chosen passage helps them move beyond such concerns.

In the first section, one student, Josh, notes right away the repetition of the word *famous* and comments that "her daughter must have emphasized this over and over." From the opening sentence, he points out that the speaker "does not sound thrilled," but he isn't sure "if it's at her daughter remarrying or the fact that her daughter doesn't feel she's good enough to meet her husband's family." Candace chooses to begin a list, anticipating some comparison/contrast of the mother and daughter. From this one passage, though, she concludes that the mother "doesn't like change" and "doesn't care for superficial things," though she "cares for her daughter." The daughter "likes keeping up with the Jones['s]" and "goes after her pie in the sky."

In the second section, Trina begins to ask questions. She does not understand the "usage" of Tan's phrase "accuses my head." She asks a more conceptual question about the end of section 2, where the mother says that her daughter speaks to her in a loud voice. Trina wonders, "Is she doing this purposely because they are with Mr. Rory, or does she really think that she has to speak to her mother like this?"

Most students begin to recognize the complexity of the story in the third section. Josh notes "duality" and the sad tone. Candace observes, "Mother: slightly depressed, slightly in wonder."

By the fourth section, students' comments are even richer. Trina recognizes the simile about the cat, "like she was threatened," and Josh notes the "oxymoron" of being "alone in this crowded beauty parlor." While some students at this point are summarizing and paraphrasing, Josh begins to synthesize; for instance, he points out that the mother and daughter are looking at one another but "still not really seeing."

In the fifth section, many of the students' anticipations are brought to fruition, and they understand the inner-versus-outer conflicts Tan is developing, especially with the mirror creating both barrier and reflection. Trina gathers more evidence for her emerging interpretation as she underlines pairs of conflicting words, noting "good" or "bad" (for happiness/sadness and good fortune/faults) and the images of present and past in the final sentence. Figure 3.1 shows two students' work as they mark up section 4.

What are the advantages of such a reading, and what happens next? If we use this reading to introduce *The Joy Luck Club*, we focus the discussion on ideas that students expect to be important to Tan in her book: mothers and daughters, quite obviously; conflict between generations; Chinese heritage and Chinese

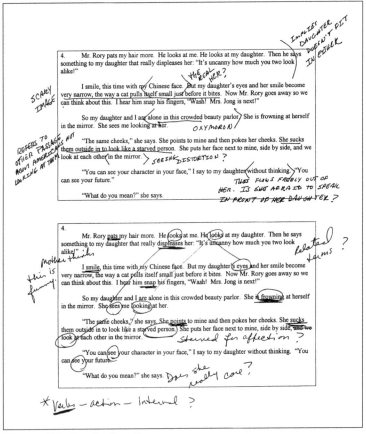

Figure 3.1. Two Student Responses

American blending; concern for appearance (and material things) versus more internal values; the desire to connect versus the desire to be different; language issues; listening versus hearing. The list goes on! But from this one exercise, which can easily be done during a forty-five- to fifty-minute class period, our students are grounding themselves in Tan's thematic world as well as gaining familiarity with her style.

Most students find this process appealing. Trina commented on this specific passage: "Each of the different sections had different emotions. If it was one longer piece, they'd all run together. This way, I read them separately." Candace, who also enjoyed the process, likened it to "analyzing a scene rather than a whole act. Then scene-by-scene, you're trying to figure out what the act is about."

As far as what comes next, the answer might well be—just read. Once students start on *The Joy Luck Club*, they'll have some ideas to look for and a sense of comfort with the author. Of course, it's always possible to give a writing assignment as a response to an interrupted reading.

■ ■ ■ ■ ■ ■ ■ ■ ■ ■ ■ ■ ■ ■ ■

Writing Assignment

Explain *how* Amy Tan conveys the struggle between the mother and daughter in this key passage from *The Joy Luck Club*.

OR

Explain the ways in which this passage predicts the major themes and conflicts in *The Joy Luck Club*.

■ ■ ■ ■ ■ ■ ■ ■ ■ ■ ■ ■ ■ ■ ■

Graphic Organizers for Character Analysis

Graphic organizers help students, especially younger readers or those unaccustomed to working with such a complex book as *The Joy Luck Club*, by providing both direction and focus—a helpful strategy given the practical reality of students' minds, which tend to stray while they read. The notes taken for graphic organizers can be useful collections of supportive evidence, which students can reflect on when doing summative writing. Also, our students often ask us to give the essay assignment when we assign the reading.

Since *The Joy Luck Club* might be characterized as a comparison/contrast book, a Venn diagram—overlapping circles—is a handy way to capture the similarities and differences between characters and then to chart the changes. Students might, for example, be asked to note the characteristics of Suyuan Woo, her daughter Jing-mei Woo, and their areas of similarity. In the first vignette, titled "The Joy Luck Club," the mother comes across as skeptical, enterprising, competitive, and relentlessly optimistic. We learn that she was a good storyteller and an enthusiastic cook. Her more tentative daughter is shy, sad, on occasion impatient, and generally disconnected, at loose ends. Even in this opening section, however, the two of them share certain traits: both are intelligent, observant, and stubborn (see Figure 3.2).

If students are assigned the Venn diagram as homework, the following day they will have something tangible to contribute to the discussion. Invariably, differences in interpretation will occur, and that's where close textual reading comes in. To debate effectively, students need to have passages and page references at hand. This might come naturally from the discussion, or an additional part of the assignment could be to note page numbers that support the characteristics students notice.

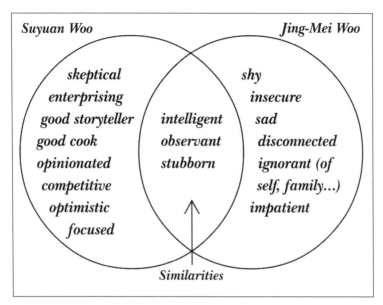

Figure 3.2. Vignette 1 "The Joy Luck Club"

Working with these two characters or any mother-daughter combination is particularly useful for two reasons. First of all, it quickly becomes clear to students that what they "know" is more reliable at some times than at others. That is, they "know" Suyuan from what others say of her, from remembered (and reported) conversations, from her actions as others recall them, and from her daughter's and friends' interpretations.

Second, students can continue developing their Venn diagrams as they read the other three vignettes about Jing-mei/June: "Two Kinds," "Best Quality," and "A Pair of Tickets." Hers is the character we see developing most fully, even more than Waverly's, and certainly most satisfactorily. By the end of the book, one could argue (and many have) that she *becomes* her mother or at least she becomes the American embodiment of the Chinese values that defined her mother. As Jing-mei develops, the middle ground of shared characteristics expands on the Venn diagram. The visual manifestation of those changes emphasizes them for students.

Close Reading in Context

As teachers, most of us engage students in close analytical reading of individual passages while we're studying a novel or play, and we expect our students to see the piece in context. An exercise that engages students in identifying specific literary elements or techniques is a good opportunity to promote active reading, just as an interrupted reading does, but in a more focused way. Although students can certainly do such close reading individually, it works well as a group exercise using a transparency or the computer. With each group responsible for marking the passage for one specific element or technique, a full markup emerges. The example below is done with different kinds of type and editing marks, but students have a good time color-coding with a transparency or on the computer.

In the passage we chose (pages 98–100 from "Rules of the Game"), Waverly and her mother are locked in an almost epic battle of wills. It's an exciting passage because Tan is bringing together the literal chess game that is the subject of the passage and the metaphorical "game" of war. We asked different groups to concentrate on words or images of (1) confinement or entrapment, (2) anger, and (3) freedom. What follows are markups from the different groups: **anger** is in bold print, <u>confinement</u> is underlined, and *freedom* is in italics. Let's look at each section as the markup emerges. First, **anger.**

> I no longer played in the alley of Waverly Place. I never visited the playground where the pigeons and old men gathered. I

went to school, then directly home to learn new chess secrets, cleverly concealed advantages, more escape routes.

But I found it **difficult to concentrate** at home. My mother had a habit of standing over me while I **plotted** out my games. I think she thought of herself as my protective ally. Her lips would be sealed tight, and after each move I made, a soft "Hmmmmmph" would escape from her nose.

Next, the students identify words and images evoking <u>confinement.</u>

I <u>no longer played</u> in the alley of Waverly Place. I <u>never visited the playground</u> where the pigeons and old men gathered. <u>I went to school, then directly home</u> to learn <u>new chess secrets,</u> cleverly concealed advantages, more escape routes.

But I found it **difficult to concentrate** at home. My mother had <u>a habit of standing over me</u> while I **plotted** out my games. I think she thought of herself as my protective ally. <u>Her lips would be sealed tight,</u> and after each move I made, a soft "Hmmmmmph" would escape from her nose.

Finally, students note words and images suggesting *freedom.*

I <u>no longer played</u> in the alley of Waverly Place. I <u>never visited the playground</u> where the *pigeons and old men gathered.* <u>I went to school, then directly home</u> to learn <u>*new chess secrets,*</u> *cleverly concealed advantages, more escape routes.*

But I found it **difficult to concentrate** at home. My mother had <u>a habit of standing over me</u> while I **plotted** out my games. I think she thought of herself as my protective ally. <u>Her lips would be sealed tight,</u> and after each move I made, a soft "Hmmmmmph" would *escape from her nose.*

One interesting outcome is that certain passages or words are marked up by more than one group. In some instances—such as "difficult to concentrate" in this passage—the point is that the language does indeed evoke more than one feeling or idea. In this case, the difficulty of concentration confines the speaker, but it also suggests anger, which, students point out, is probably the reason for her difficulty concentrating.

In other instances, the double marking results from disagreement about meaning. Some students felt the "new chess secrets" were an avenue of freedom for Waverly, while others argued that the very concept of "secret" is a type of entrapment. The point is not necessarily to resolve such debate but to allow it to animate and enlarge the discussion.

We use this process of small-group discussion followed by whole-class discussion to encourage students to develop their own essay topics. After going through this exercise, for instance, students notice on their own the correlation between the chess moves on the board and those in life. They start to develop their own approaches to writing about this book, often more creative topics than teacher-generated ones. Two that emerged after this exercise were Waverly's internal battle between acceding to her mother's wishes and asserting her independence (a stretch, granted), and the mother's inevitable struggle to hold on to her daughter even as she realizes the need to let her go.

Following is a full markup of the passage with elements from all three groups.

Close Reading

I <u>no longer played</u> in the alley of Waverly Place. I <u>never visited the playground</u> where the *pigeons and old men gathered*. <u>I went to school, then directly home</u> to learn <u>*new chess secrets*</u>, *cleverly concealed advantages, more escape routes.*

But I found it **difficult to concentrate** at home. My mother had <u>a habit of standing over me</u> while I **plotted** out my games.

I think she thought of herself as my protective ally. <u>Her lips would be sealed tight,</u> and after each move I made, a soft "Hmmmmmph" would *escape from her nose.*

"Ma, I can't practice when you stand there like that," I said one day. She <u>retreated</u> to the kitchen and made loud noises with the pots and pans. When the **crashing** stopped, I could see out of the corner of my eye that she was <u>standing in the doorway.</u> "Hmmmph!" <u>Only this one came out of her</u> **tight throat.**

My parents made many concessions to allow me to practice. One time I complained that the bedroom I shared was so noisy that I couldn't think. Thereafter, my brothers <u>slept in a bed in the living room facing the street</u>. I said I couldn't finish my rice; my head didn't work right when my stomach was too full. I left the table with half-finished bowls and nobody complained. But there was <u>one duty I couldn't avoid</u>. I had to accompany my mother on Saturday market days when I had no tournament to play. My mother would proudly walk with me, visiting many shops, buying very little. "This my daughter Wave-ly Jong," she said to whoever looked her way.

One day, after we left a shop I **said under my breath**, "I wish you wouldn't do that, telling everybody I'm your daughter." My mother stopped walking. <u>Crowds of people with heavy bags pushed past us on the sidewalk, bumping into first one shoulder, then another.</u>

"Aiii-ya. So shame be with mother?" She **grasped** <u>my hand even tighter</u> as she **glared** at me.

I looked down. "It's not that, it's just so obvious. It's just so embarrassing."

"Embarrass you be my daughter?" Her voice was **cracking with anger**.

"That's not what I meant. That's not what I said."

"What you say?"

<u>I knew it was a mistake to say anything more</u>, but I heard my voice speaking. "Why do you have to use me to show off? If you want to show off, then why don't you learn to play chess."

My mother's eyes turned into **dangerous black slits**. She had no words for me, just **sharp silence**.

I felt the *wind rushing* around my hot ears. I **jerked** my hand out of my mother's **tight grasp and spun around, knocking** into an old woman. *Her bag of groceries spilled to the ground.*

"Aii-ya! Stupid girl!" my mother and the woman cried. Oranges and tin cans *careened* down the sidewalk. As my mother stooped to help the old woman pick up *the escaping food, I took off.*

I raced down the street, *dashing between people, not looking back* as my mother **screamed shrilly**, "Meimei! Meimei!" I fled <u>down an alley, past dark curtained shops and merchants washing the grime off their windows</u>. *I sped into the sunlight*, into a large street <u>crowded with tourists</u> examining trinkets and souvenirs. I <u>ducked into another dark alley, down another street, up another alley. I ran until it hurt and I realized I had nowhere to go, that I was not running from anything. The alleys contained no escape routes.</u>

My breath came out **like angry smoke. It was cold**. I sat down on an upturned plastic pail next to a stack of empty boxes, cupping my chin with my hands, thinking hard. I imagined my mother, first walking briskly down one street or another looking for me, then giving up and returning home to await my arrival. After two hours, I stood up on <u>creaking legs and slowly walked home</u>.

The alley was quiet and I could see the yellow lights shining from our flat like <u>two tiger's eyes in the night</u>. I climbed the sixteen steps to the door, advancing quietly up each so as not to make any warning sounds. I turned the knob; <u>the door was locked</u>. I heard a chair moving, quick steps, the locks turning—click! click! click!—*and then the door opened*.

"About time you got home," said Vincent. "Boy, are you in trouble."

He slid back to the dinner table. On a platter were the remains of a large fish, its <u>fleshy head still connected to bones swimming upstream in vain escape</u>. Standing there waiting for my punishment, I heard my mother speak in a **dry voice**.

"We not concerning this girl. This girl not have concerning for us."

Nobody looked at me. Bone chopsticks **clinked against the**

insides of bowls <u>being emptied into hungry mouths.</u>

I walked into my room, <u>closed the door,</u> and lay down on my bed. <u>The room was dark, the ceiling filled with shadows from the dinnertime lights of neighboring flats.</u>

In my head, I saw a chessboard with sixty-four black and white squares. Opposite me was my opponent, two angry black slits. She wore a triumphant smile. "*Strongest wind cannot be seen,*" she said.

Her black men advanced across the plane, slowly marching to each successive level as a single unit. My white pieces **screamed** as they scurried and fell off the board one by one. *As her men drew closer to my edge, I felt myself growing light. I rose up into the air and flew out the window. Higher and higher, above the alley, over the tops of tiled roofs, where I was gathered up by the wind and pushed up toward the night sky until everything below me disappeared and I was alone.*

<u>I closed my eyes</u> and <u>*pondered my next move.*</u>

4 Meeting the Challenges of *The Joy Luck Club*

■ ■

The Joy Luck Club has enjoyed commercial success as well as literary staying power—with good reason. It's a rich and engaging book with themes both culturally specific and universal, such as parent-child conflict, immigration and assimilation, identity formation, and even the pursuit of the American dream. But it's not an easy work, and both structure and context pose challenges for teachers and students alike. As we discussed our own experiences with the book, we decided to tap into the rich learning community of local colleagues who teach *The Joy Luck Club*. Through e-mail and conversation, we identified four challenges:

- A problematic narrative structure
- Eight complex characters
- Unfamiliar cultural context
- Gender bias

With a little help from our English teacher friends, we found a creative range of strategies and solutions to address each of these issues.

Problematic Narrative Structure

In Chapter 2, we explain how we usually work with the structure of *The Joy Luck Club*, but some of our colleagues prefer to restructure the book. That makes sense since Amy Tan wrote it as a series of short stories. In fact, when the publishers were designing the cover and wanted to call it a "novel," Tan objected, and they settled on a book jacket description of "fiction." Tan points out that she was, in fact, a bit embarrassed by an early review praising her "clever and innovative structure": "Imagine how disappointed the reviewer would have been if I had told him that the structure of this so-called novel was instead the result of a more eclectic arrangement of sixteen *short stories*" (*Opposite of Fate* 304).

In "Required Reading and Other Dangerous Subjects," Tan reacts to some of her readers' theories about the structure of the book. She comments on a master's thesis she read in which the author emphasizes Tan's use of the number four at least "thirty-two or thirty-six times" (*Opposite of Fate* 300). This writer points out "four mothers, four daughters, four sections of the book, four stories per section, . . . four sides to a mah jong table, four directions of the wind, four players" (300). Tan seems amused by this type of analysis, insisting that she's not nearly as clever as some of her readers believe: "I don't claim my use of the number four to be a brilliant symbolic device. . . . I consider my *overuse* of the number four to be a flaw" (301).

Tan planned at first to have five sections with three stories for each of the five elements (earth, fire, wood, water, and metal), but her agent discouraged her. While contracted to produce sixteen stories, Tan worried that she would be short of the required word count she had agreed to. Instead, she produced seventeen stories, but her editor, Faith Sale, felt that one of the stories did not belong, so the number of stories was reduced. Sale suggested that the sixteen stories be reordered, and that's when Tan proposed that the structure be "an emotional one, linked by a small fable," as discussed in Chapter 2.

We talked with colleagues who have found a range of ways to address the four-by-four structure that is complicated by shifts in time, place, and narrator. Specifically, they use groups to focus on specific stories or restructure the reading to emphasize the mother-daughter pairings.

Group Presentations

Janet Slade Young from Springbrook High School in Silver Spring, Maryland, divides the text in half. She assigns the first eight stories (with a reading schedule) for discussion and the second eight stories as a group project. Each of eight groups is assigned one story and makes a presentation on plot, character development, and custom. In addition, each group creates a poster about its story, incorporating significant ideas and elements. Ms. Young keeps a photograph book of her students presenting their posters to the class. She saves some of the best ones as models for her next year's students.

Mothers' Stories/Daughters' Stories: Pairing

Several teachers restructure *The Joy Luck Club* according to mother-daughter pairings to help students focus on the *complete* narrative of each character in the book (see Table 4.1). When Tan worked on the screenplay of the film, this is the approach that she and her co-writers took (see Chapter 5). In addition, such restructuring highlights differences between the mothers' lives (in China and as immigrants) and the daughters' lives (as Chinese Americans in the United States).

Each pair of stories the mothers tell is a narrative about their memories of life in China, and some expand to include memories of their own mothers and their daughters. Note that Suyuan's story is the only one not directly told but embedded in other stories.

Table 4.1

Mother	Stories
Suyuan Woo	"The Joy Luck Club" and "A Pair of Tickets" Since Suyuan is dead when the book begins, her stories are embedded in Jing-mei's. "The Joy Luck Club" tells about her flight from Kweilin and loss of all her possessions. "A Pair of Tickets" continues her stories through her husband's voice as she reveals her decision to abandon her babies and her lifelong search to find them.
An-mei Hsu	"Scar" and "Magpies" "Scar" details An-mei at age four when her mother returns to her grandmother's house. "Magpies" continues the story of An-mei's mother and An-mei's decision to live with her mother five years later.
Lindo Jong	"The Red Candle" and "Double Face" "The Red Candle" explores Lindo's arranged marriage and her release from it. "Double Face" continues her story as she leaves China, makes her way to the United States, remarries, and begins her own family.
Ying-ying St. Clair	"The Moon Lady" and "Waiting between the Trees" "The Moon Lady" tells about Ying-ying at age four during a celebration of the Moon Festival. "Waiting between the Trees" continues with her life, starting at age sixteen, her difficult first marriage, and her second marriage to St. Clair.

The daughters' paired stories explore their childhood memories and their relationships with their mothers (both as children and as adults), and some reflect on their relationships with one another or with husbands or lovers (see Table 4.2).

Table 4.2

Daughter	Stories
Jing-mei Woo	"The Joy Luck Club," "Two Kinds," "Best Quality," and "A Pair of Tickets" (June is the only character to appear in all four sections.) "The Joy Luck Club" explains the mahjong club, June's replacement of her mother in the club, and the discovery of her long-lost sisters in China. In "Two Kinds," June remembers her attempts to play the piano as a child. "Best Quality" depicts June as a young adult at the time her mother gives her a jade pendant, her "life's importance." The final story about June, "A Pair of Tickets," concerns June's journey to China to meet her sisters, the twins her mother abandoned many years earlier.
Rose Hsu Jordan	"Half and Half" and "Without Wood" As Rose prepares for her divorce from her husband Ted, she remembers in "Half and Half" the death of her younger brother and her mother's attempts to fight fate. Rose continues her story in "Without Wood" as she asserts herself with her husband and decides to hold on to her house rather than sell it.
Waverly Jong	"Rules of the Game" and "Four Directions" Waverly tells about herself as a childhood chess prodigy in "Rules of the Game." "Four Directions" explores Waverly's impending second marriage to an American man and her attempts to have her mother approve of him.
Lena St. Clair	"The Voice from the Wall" and "Rice Husband" "The Voice from the Wall" depicts Lena's childhood memories of her mother's sorrow at losing a child. In "Rice Husband," Lena's story continues with her marriage to Harold and their cold "50-50" relationship.

A reorganization of the book by pairing the mother-daughter stories shifts the emphasis to the intergenerational relationships and conflicts. Sally Lucas from Damascus High School in Damascus, Maryland, uses the families as the organizational frame for her classroom. She divides her class into four family groups, and each group presents information about its "stories" to the class (see Table 4.3).

Complex Characters

Certainly a teacher wrestling with the structure of the book will also be challenged to help students distinguish the characters from one another. Some of our students face difficulties not only pronouncing names but also perceiving differences among the four

Table 4.3

Mother-Daughter Pair	Stories
The Woo family Suyuan and Jing-mei	"The Joy Luck Club" "Two Kinds" "Best Quality" "A Pair of Tickets"
The Hsu family An-mei and Waverly	"Scar" "Half and Half" "Without Wood" "Magpies"
The Jong family Lindo and Waverly	"The Red Candle" "Rules of the Game" "Four Directions" "Double Face"
The St. Clair family Ying-ying and Lena	"The Moon Lady" "The Voice from the Wall" "Rice Husband" "Waiting between the Trees"

mothers and the daughters. The following strategies may be helpful in addressing this difficulty.

Role-Playing

We've had success in assigning students to role-play characters in a novel or short story. (Depending on the size of the class, several students can be assigned to role-play the same character.) For *The Joy Luck Club*, we ask students to *become* An-mei or Lindo or Ying-ying. This role-playing task can be accomplished in panel discussions (the mothers, the daughters, and additional minor characters) or with individual characters taking the stage for a class period or part of a class period. The rest of the class develops questions to ask each character. The role-players must answer in character (some even go so far as to try to speak with an accent or wear a simple costume) based on the content of the stories. It's also useful for someone to play the role of the author or perhaps an "off-stage" character (such as June's father or Amy Tan's mother). Sometimes students have trouble initially going from third person to the first-person "I," but navigating this change is actually part of the learning process.

Ultimately, students distinguish the characters much more clearly using this role-playing strategy. They must complete a deep reading of the text (both the role-players and the questioners) and get to know a character from the inside out before they can speak *as* the character. The voices of the characters truly come alive in the classroom. Imagine, for instance, starting with a question about an issue in the text: "Jing-mei, do you think your mother is responsible for your feelings of insecurity?" or "Lena, do you love your husband?" But questions can also extend beyond the text, as long as the students remain in character. So, for instance, "Waverly, how would you describe your mother to your daughter

Shoshana?" Or, "Ms. Tan, why did you title that section 'American Translation'?"

Vignette Sheets

Emily Sigman from Wootton High School in Rockville, Maryland, found that keeping characters straight was the single-most difficult task for her tenth graders, so she developed the chart in Figure 4.1 to help them focus on the character relationships, especially the conflicts, as they read the stories.

The Joy Luck Club: Ms. Sigman

Section Heading:
Vignette Title:
Location:
Main Characters:
Describe the relationships between the characters:

Conflicts:
            Internal   External

Lesson learned by character(s)

Universal Lesson

Figure 4.1

Judith Smith from Montgomery Blair High School, Silver Spring, Maryland, uses a similar strategy to help her students differentiate characters. She might begin with just the characters' names and allow the students to fill in the remainder of the grid. This is a variation on note taking, one that requires students to make connections, synthesize, and create a visually logical summary. Dr. Smith's table with sample responses is shown in Table 4.4.

Dr. Smith also gives quizzes about characters: she asks students to match the character to the event or action in the text or to match characters and quotations. As a summative assignment and another way to help students distinguish among the characters, she gives the following writing assignment based on the character relationships explored in the book.

■ ■ ■ ■ ■ ■ ■ ■ ■ ■ ■ ■ ■ ■ ■ ■ ■

Writing Assignment

Amy Tan's *The Joy Luck Club* paradoxically takes as central issues the strength of the mother-daughter bond as well as the inevitable conflicts that develop between mothers and their daughters. Write a well-developed essay on this conflict-filled connection between three mothers and their daughters in *The Joy Luck Club*. Choose among An-mei Hsu and Rose, Ying-ying St. Clair and Lena, Suyuan Woo and Jing-mei (June), and Lindo Jong and Waverly.

■ ■ ■ ■ ■ ■ ■ ■ ■ ■ ■ ■ ■ ■ ■ ■ ■

Unfamiliar Cultural Context

Most students benefit from some attention to the cultural contexts of *The Joy Luck Club*, whether the history of China, immigra-

Table 4.4

Mother	Stories	Events/Actions
Suyuan Woo	"The Joy Luck Club" "A Pair of Tickets"	Starts the JLC. Leaves her daughters on the road. Seeks reunion with daughters.
An-mei Hsu	"Scar" "Magpies"	Sees her mother's sacrifice for her mother/daughter. Learns how her mother was manipulated into servitude. Loses Bing.
Lindo Jong	"The Red Candle" "Double Face"	Forced into marriage. Tricks her way out. Suffers domination by mother-in-law. Tries to acculturate to America.
Ying-ying St. Clair	"The Moon Lady" "Waiting between the Trees"	Spoiled child lost and found. Forced first marriage. Loveless cross-cultural second marriage.

Daughter	Chapters	Event/Actions
Jing-mei (June) Woo	"Two Kinds" "Best Quality" "A Pair of Tickets"	False piano prodigy. Defeated by Waverly. Reunited with her sisters in China.
Rose Hsu Jordan	"Half and Half" "Without Wood"	Divorce from Ted. Loss of mother's faith. Loss of brother Bing. Struggle to assert self.
Waverly Jong	"Rules of the Game" "Four Directions"	Chess champion. War with mother. Tries to get mother to accept marriage to Rich. Deals with Rich's insensitivity.
Lena St. Clair	"The Voice from the Wall" "Rice Husband"	Mother's mental illness. Conflict with Harold over money.

tion policies and patterns in the United States, or traditions related to food and marriage customs. "In "Required Reading and Other Dangerous Subjects," Tan says she worries that "if you are a minority, you may not be read in the same way that, say, Anne Tyler, John Updike, or Sue Grafton is read. . . . [Y]our stories may not be read as literary fiction, or as American fiction, or as entertainment; they will be read more likely as sociology, politics, ideology, cultural lesson plans in a narrative form" (*Opposite of Fate* 308). It seems reasonable to us, however, to acknowledge that *The Joy Luck Club* has a specific cultural context that is essential to it even though we by no means devalue its artistry—or neglect its more universal themes.

The Mahjong Game

This game is important to the book, even lending it its title. In "The Joy Luck Club," the first story, June remembers her mother's explanation of how the club began "on a summer night that was so hot even the moths fainted to the ground," when she had the idea of inviting three other women to meet weekly. Each, she says, "would host a party to raise money and to raise our spirits" (23).

> "So we decided to hold parties and pretend each week had become the new year. Each week we could forget past wrongs done to us. We weren't allowed to think a bad thought. We feasted, we laughed, we played games, lost and won, we told the best stories. And each week, we could hope to be lucky. That hope was our only joy. And that's how we came to call our little parties Joy Luck." (25)

Teachers may have students in their classes or school who are familiar with the game and willing to give a quick introductory lesson or overview; a number of Web sites also give instructions on how to play mahjong. In addition, materials from The Center for Learning suggest the following activity about mahjong to help students understand how it functions symbolically in *The Joy Luck Club*:

Mahjong Activity

1. The East Wind always starts round 1. The other corners of the table are the other winds. For all other hands, a throw of the dice determines who will start. The order differs every time.
2. The person who is the prevailing wind rolls the dice and counts out the location of a break in the "wall" of tiles.
3. The game ends when one player's hand is complete. All the other players have incomplete hands.
4. Explain any parallels you see [with *The Joy Luck Club*].

(© The Center for Learning by Jayne R. Smith)

Traditional Chinese Poetry

We list in Chapter 1 a number of poems that explore parent-child relationships, but we also like pairing *The Joy Luck Club* with traditional Chinese poetry. A wealth of Web sites offers examples, both in translation and in Chinese, to help students understand the connections between Tan's book and the poetic experience. Students could, for example, make connections between the following poem, "Remembrance" by Su Dongpo (www.chinapage.org/poem2e.html), and write about how these words express the feelings and experiences of An-mei Hsu or Suyuan Woo:

> To what can our life on earth be likened?
> To a flock of geese
> alighting on the snow.
> Sometimes leaving a trace of their passage.

We are particularly fond of former U.S. Poet Laureate Billy Collins's wonderful poem "Reading an Anthology of Chinese Poems of the Sung Dynasty, I Pause to Admire the Length and Clarity of Their Titles" (www.americanpoems.com/poets/Billy_Collins/812). Collins quotes full and lengthy titles of several traditional Chinese poems. Is there a connection between these titles that Collins writes about and Tan's fable titles (those that introduce each of the sections of the book)? Does a title such as "Waiting between the Trees" help a reader "enter" into the story, as Collins suggests in his poem?

Cultural Practices and Customs

The Joy Luck Club can be read through a cultural lens as students learn customs related to food, marriage, and dress. Likewise, they explore the role and status of women in China prior to the Cultural Revolution. Following are excerpts from an essay written by Samantha Schilit, a tenth grader at Wootton High School, who synthesizes and interprets ideas about cultural practices from the book. In a conventional essay, this young student demonstrates her control of a thesis, her ability to draw inferences from the text, and her skill using quotations as support. Essentially, she is explaining what the book taught her about a particular culture.

> In Amy Tan's classic novel, *The Joy Luck Club*, the cultural context of the mothers' upbringings is portrayed through the depiction of mother-daughter relationships, the roles of women, and marriage customs in the third vignette, "The Red Candle."
>
> Tan portrays the cultural context of the novel through mother-daughter relationships, specifically through familial responsibility and value for loyalty and tradition. One Chinese familial responsibility is the obligation of raising and giving up an obedient and courteous daughter. Lindo Jong's mother nurtures her daughter by telling her that a daughter without man-

ners possesses "such an ugly face [that] the Huang's won't want her" (Tan 45). Although this sounds heartless, Lindo's mother truly loves her daughter, but she is trying to make the separation easier because she knows it is her responsibility to give up her daughter. As Lindo passes from the care of her mother to that of the Huangs, she "learns to be polite with [them], especially Huang Taitai" (46), as that is what is expected of a devoted wife and daughter in law. Her loyalty to a sense of family and tradition enables her to respect any relatives, no matter how distant or close. . . .

Tan details marriage customs in order to portray the cultural context of the novel. By the time Lindo is two years old, "the village matchmaker [had already come] to [her] family" and determined Lindo's value and suitability for Huang Taitai's son. This reveals two important aspects about this culture: lineage is more important than character, and individuals have no self-determination over their fate. The depiction of marriage customs also indicates that symbolism is very important. The covenant between Lindo and Tyuan-yu is represented by "a red candle [that is] supposed to seal [their marriage] forever" (55). In this culture, the belief is that certain symbols bind people to marriage and are truly sanctified. Through the marriage customs that Lindo encounters, such as the family involvement, her value as determined by her lineage, and the symbolism of the red candle, Tan illustrates the cultural background of the novel.

—*Samantha Schilit*

Many teachers we spoke with tap into the cultural experiences and knowledge of Chinese friends, Chinese colleagues, or Chinese students in their classes or school when teaching this book. Sally Lucas at Damascus High School brings in a scrapbook of materials that she collected when she visited China, including money, pictures of herself by the Great Wall, and other artifacts. And, of course, there's always Chinese food to enrich any discussion. One brief but creative activity we have used is to ask students to imagine that they have just gotten their first writing job—writing the fortunes that will go into Chinese fortune cookies, particularly in light of the amusing passage in *The Joy Luck Club*:

> "What is this nonsense?" I [Lindo] asked her, putting the strips of paper in my pocket, thinking I should study these classical American sayings.
>
> "They are fortunes," she [An-mei] explained. "American people think Chinese people write these things."
>
> "But we never say such things!" I said. "These things don't make sense. They are not fortunes, they are bad instructions."
>
> "No, miss," she said, laughing, "it is our bad fortune to be here making these and somebody else's bad fortune to pay to get them." (262)

Ask students to write out their best examples of fortunes and share them with the class. Follow up with a fortune cookie snack and make connections with the ideas of good fortune and luck (or even bad luck) that are evident in *The Joy Luck Club*.

Connections to the Students' Own Cultural Heritage

Two teachers, Julie Zaldumbide and Sally Lucas, both at Damascus High School, use activities in their classrooms to make connections between students' cultural heritages and the cultural heritage explored in Tan's book. Ms. Zaldumbide begins by sharing a story of her own Irish heritage and then asks students to give short speeches about some significant event or experience from their own culture. Ms. Lucas uses a similar speech activity and asks students to share their personal heritage with their classmates.

Ms. Young focuses on the idea that heritage is a gift passed from one generation to another. She reviews the first fable in *The

Joy Luck Club, about the mother's desire to pass on the swan feather to her daughter, a symbol of her good intentions. Ms. Young asks students to bring an item to class that they would pass to the next generation and explain their selection.

Gender Bias

Tan takes a strong position on issues related to women in the literary canon. She recalls her life as an English major in 1970 and the works she studied in her American literature classes. In "Required Reading and Other Dangerous Subjects," she states that she rarely read women or minority writers: "During those years that I was an English major, the only female novelist I read was Virginia Woolf" (*Opposite of Fate* 318). When she finally resumed reading fiction fifteen years later, she "mostly read fiction by women" because, she says, "I had so rarely read novels by women in my adult years, and I found I enjoyed their sensibilities, their voices, and what they had to say about the world. . . . I kept reading, day and night, until I couldn't stop myself from *writing*" (319).

In an interview in *Poets & Writers Magazine*, she comments on the absence of strong male voices in *The Joy Luck Club* and explains this in terms of her artistic vision:

> I kept thinking that I should have more balance, that I should put some strong male figure in there. Then I said, "No, you have to stay focused on what this book is about. You have to make some choices." That is a flaw in the book, but for me to correct the flaw would have thrown the book in another direction, and I couldn't do it at that point. The men are in there almost as pawns for bringing up the conflicts between the mothers and daughters; that's sort of unfortunate.
> I don't think of the men as being as unsympathetic as a lot of people see them. People always say, "The men are weak,"

but really many of them by other standards are very strong men. The flaw, the weakness, is that we only see the moment in the relationship when they are seen as not that sympathetic. I think there are other dimensions to those men that I could have enlarged upon to make them more sympathetic, but it would have made the book lopsided in another sense. (Somogyi and Stanton 29)

Such context is interesting, but it doesn't change the fact that many of our male students call *The Joy Luck Club* "chick lit" in a somewhat derogatory tone. Perhaps there's not much we can do except to acknowledge that this label is one some might give the book. One of our colleagues says she reminds her students of the many other books they've read in class in which the dominant characters are male (e.g., *All Quiet on the Western Front*, *The Odyssey*, *Lord of the Flies*). Another teacher told us that gender was not a big issue in her classroom because she reminds the boys who voice this concern that they all have mothers, some have sisters, many have extended families of grandmothers and aunts, and many have girlfriends. What better way to understand women than to read about them!

■ ■ ■ ■ ■ ■ ■ ■ ■ ■ ■ ■ ■ ■ ■

Writing Assignment

Write a description of one of the female characters from the point of view of one of the male characters. For example, have June's father describe his marriage to Suyuan or Harold describe whether he believes his wife Lena is like her mother.

■ ■ ■ ■ ■ ■ ■ ■ ■ ■ ■ ■ ■ ■ ■

5 The Art of Film: *The Joy Luck Club* on Screen

■ ■

> I've now seen the movie about twenty-five times, and I am not
> ashamed to say I've been moved to tears each time. ("*Joy Luck*
> and Hollywood," *Opposite of Fate* 202)

So says Amy Tan about her experience of seeing the film that was
made of her book *The Joy Luck Club*. We agree that the film is
powerful and affords students an opportunity to see a novel they've
studied come to life on the screen and to witness the author's
hand in shaping its creation. It's another way to engage students
in analysis of the novel, critical thinking, and even close reading
of the written text.

The Joy Luck Club on screen has other advantages. Amy Tan
was one of the principal writers for the screenplay. Many members of the real Joy Luck Club and their friends auditioned for the
film and were cast as extras. Tan's niece won a coveted speaking
part, and her aunt and uncle played dinner guests in the scene in
which Waverly's boyfriend douses the meal with soy sauce. Even
Tan's mother was an extra in the opening party scene. And, like
Hitchcock's clever cameos in each of his films, Tan herself appears in the opening scene with fellow screenwriter Ron Bass.
They walk into the party and apologize for their late arrival.

Why Teach Film At All?

When it comes to using film in the classroom, English teachers typically fall into two camps: those who rely on a video when they need to be away from the classroom and those who believe there is too much to accomplish in the classroom with all the literature they have to teach (and the writing and the grammar and the speaking and . . .) and just not enough time to incorporate film into their work. We'd like to suggest an alternative viewpoint, one that falls somewhere in the middle of these two perspectives—that film belongs in the English classroom as a way to enrich the study of any work of literature, particularly a film as good as *The Joy Luck Club*.

In *Reel Conversations: Reading Film with Young Adults*, authors Teasley and Wilder present a rationale for including film study in the English classroom (4–7). They acknowledge that

- Students have prior, positive experiences with film.
- Film is already used in classrooms anyway (and frequently in ways that are a disservice to film).
- Film is a form of art that deserves a place in the curriculum.
- Film viewing provides rich opportunities for discussion and writing.
- Nonprint media is a growing area of interest in the English classroom.

Similarly, William V. Costanzo, in *Reading the Movies: Twelve Great Films on Video and How to Teach Them* and in his subsequent book *Great Films and How to Teach Them*, notes the broad view of NCTE's Commission on Media in including film and other media in its definition of literacy. Costanzo discusses "the information culture" and argues that students need to develop an appreciation of film along with the ability to analyze and criticize written texts.

He concludes that "[t]hese are favorable times, then, to bring movies into the mainstream of education, to make film study part of the ongoing curriculum" (*Reading the Movies* 3). In addition, Amy Tan's direct involvement and belief in the film of her book lend credibility to the adaptation and changes the book undergoes on the screen.

In the pages that follow, we discuss a number of approaches to *The Joy Luck Club*-the-film, but we never use all of them in the classroom. We always use film clips and some scene analysis, but the extent of our use of this film (as well as others) depends on the class level, where in the school year *The Joy Luck Club* is studied, student interest, and other individual classroom issues. To make it easier to select scenes, at the end of this chapter we have provided a summary of the ten scenes in the DVD version of the film.

Tan and Hollywood: A Creative Collaboration

Tan admits in "*Joy Luck* and Hollywood" (*Opposite of Fate*) that she "was an unlikely person to get involved with filmmaking. . . . I've always preferred to daydream about characters of my own making. At the same time, I didn't hold any grudges against movies as an art form" (176). She was simply "neither fan nor foe" (176). She elaborates on how she became involved in making the film version of *The Joy Luck Club* in a chronology that she calls "The Blow by Blow" (180–83).

Shortly after the book was published, Tan met director Wayne Wang and realized that he was the right person to direct a movie of *The Joy Luck Club* if one was ever made, and in 1990 they formed a collaborative team with screenwriter Ronald Bass. All three agreed on two primary conditions: that they would work and write collaboratively and that they would insist on creative control.

Although one early contract fell through (because Tan was not given the creative control she wanted), Disney Studio chair Jeffrey Katzenberg and Kathryn Galan and Henry Huang of Hollywood Pictures read the narrative version of the script; agreed on the creative control that Tan, Wang, and Bass wanted; and filming began in 1992.

Although their work styles were dramatically different, Tan, Wang, and Bass worked effectively to collaborate on the script for *The Joy Luck Club*. Tan notes that after three days, the three writers had a narrative version of the script. She created the first draft, Bass revised it, and "then [they] would revise each other, making sure [they] agreed on every single word, especially in dialogue" (*Opposite of Fate* 186). Tan describes this process as something like a "relay race" (186). In fact, the "collaboration was so thorough that by the time we saw screenings of the movie, we often could not remember who had written what" (186). The three writers handled differences by each taking on a specific role. Tan was "the arbiter of character questions," Bass handled "overall structure and emotional truth," and Wang became the "final arbiter on everything, because he was, after all, the director" (187–88).

In an interview, Wayne Wang explains *The Joy Luck Club*'s attraction for him: "When I was given Amy Tan's book, I read it, and found it very moving. . . . [T]he stories reminded me of stories I heard while growing up" (Tibbetts 2). His favorite scene in the film is when Waverly's American boyfriend makes faux pas after faux pas during a dinner with Waverly's parents: "When I read [the story], I remembered different things in my own background where a Caucasian had to cope with the Chinese 'Emily Post' kind of things. It's funny how such small details of table etiquette can create such serious problems!" (2). Wang also comments that the film captures the range of experiences of his parents' generation, the responsibility his generation has to learn from the past, and the burden of expectations that parents pass on to their children.

Although as teachers we like to provide background similar to the information just discussed, we also like to give students a way to approach the film on their own.

■ ■ ■ ■ ■ ■ ■ ■ ■ ■ ■ ■ ■ ■ ■ ■

Discussion Assignment
List five favorite films and explain briefly why you've chosen these particular ones. What makes a film "good"? Share your lists and criteria for "good."

■ ■ ■ ■ ■ ■ ■ ■ ■ ■ ■ ■ ■ ■ ■ ■

A Word to the Wise: R Rating

Clearly, a film version of this book in which the author is so intimately involved deserves some classroom viewing time. But this is also a cautionary tale, because the film of *The Joy Luck Club* is rated R, which disqualifies a film for classroom viewing in most public high schools. The film contains some expletives (probably nothing a high school student hasn't already heard), sexually explicit scenes, a rape, infanticide, and a suicide. In her essay "*Joy Luck* and Hollywood," Tan discusses how Ron Bass and Wayne Wang wrote the sex scene. She says that including the sex scene was a decision Bass and Wang reached, and that she worried the scene "was an automatic red flag for exploitation and gratuitous thrills" (*Opposite of Fate* 188). Bass and Wang prevailed, however, although Tan did not participate in the writing of the scene itself.

In retrospect, she claims, "that was the best time I had not writing something. And now that the scene is on the screen, I'm rather fond of it" (189).

So, how can a classroom teacher use the film productively and wisely in the classroom? We talked with a number of teachers who told us that they use the entire film without hesitation and have never had any complaints or concerns. But we prefer film clips, not only because they avoid rating problems but also because they contribute to student thinking, discussing, and writing about the book and the film. Plus, using film clips minimizes the time away from written text.

1. Use a film clip to introduce characters

Our colleague Sally Lucas uses a film clip to introduce the characters in the book before assigning the reading to her students. She believes that these clips help her students to distinguish each character and can provide a clear visual image students can carry with them as they read. We recommend two clips as excellent introductions to the characters.

Film Viewing Activity

Show the opening party scene of the film. As each character enters the shot, provide introductions to your students. Say, for example, "The three women sitting at the table are the Aunties, Lindo, An-mei, and Ying-ying."

OR

Show the final shots of the film (before the closing credits)—two still photographs. (Freeze the frame.) The first photograph poses the four mothers and the four daughters. Introduce the characters to your students. Then show the second photograph. Have students identify the characters. Ask students which character is missing. Have students predict why that character (Suyuan Woo) does not appear in the second photograph.

■ ■ ■ ■ ■ ■ ■ ■ ■ ■ ■ ■ ■ ■ ■ ■ ■

2. Use film clips as companions to textual analysis

A wonderful follow-up to a close textual analysis such as the interrupted reading activity we explored in Chapter 3 is to do a similar close textual reading of a film clip. Try, for example, scene 3 in the DVD of *The Joy Luck Club*, Waverly's story. This scene is quite complex, with many levels of flashback. It begins with a phone call between Waverly and her mother and their plans to meet at a beauty parlor where Waverly has arranged for a makeover for her mother. The scene continues with a conversation between Waverly and the hair stylist while her mother sits in the chair. Waverly talks about her mother as if she does not comprehend the conversation. The scene segues into a flashback using a marvelous technique: Lindo is pumped down in the salon chair and gradually disappears from the frame. The flashbacks that follow depict Waverly showing her mother a new fur coat that her boyfriend Rich has given her, a dinner scene at Lindo's house where Rich makes a number of mistakes in Chinese etiquette, followed by a short sequence with Waverly and Rich in the car driving home from the dinner. The scene returns to the beauty parlor, continuing to explore the growing tension between Waverly and Lindo.

■ ■ ■ ■ ■ ■ ■ ■ ■ ■ ■ ■ ■ ■ ■ ■ ■

Film Analysis Activity I

View this final section of scene 3 *without sound*. Take notes on the visual images the scene explores.

■ How does the camera show the relationship between Waverly and her mother?

■ What objects in the scene (mise-en-scène) help to develop the relationship between Waverly and Lindo?

■ How do costumes and color help to develop character?

■ How does the additional flashback scene between Lindo and her mother connect to the present scene in the beauty parlor?

■ What kind of emotional elements are developed by the actions of the characters?

■ ■ ■ ■ ■ ■ ■ ■ ■ ■ ■ ■ ■ ■ ■ ■ ■

Students will see from the silent film clip that although Waverly and her mother occupy the same frame in the scene, they never speak directly to each other; they speak instead to their images reflected in the beauty parlor mirrors.

■ ■ ■ ■ ■ ■ ■ ■ ■ ■ ■ ■ ■ ■ ■ ■ ■

Film Analysis Activity II

View the same film clip *with sound*. Pay attention to the dialogue that develops between Lindo and Waverly. A number of particularly powerful lines continue to reveal their relationship. Lindo states early in the film clip that her daughter is "looking but not seeing" and that she fears

Waverly is "ashamed" of her. When Lindo begins to remember her own mother brushing her hair, she begins to cry, causing Waverly to feel uncomfortable. Waverly also confesses that her mother has "power" over her, "one word, one look." When she adds that "nothing can please [her mother]," her mother's response is "Now you make me happy." With that comment, the two women look into the mirror and begin to laugh. They've reached an emotional breakthrough in their relationship. (In this scene, they both cry and laugh.) Consider how the film clip with sound reinforces the elements you noted when you watched without sound.

■■■■■■■■■■■■■■■■■

After this viewing, students fairly easily make a connection to the title of the original story in the book, "Double Face."

3. Use film clips for scene analysis

Another activity using film clips in the classroom that we've found effective is having students view a particular scene for close analysis. Sometime we use one of the scene sequences in the DVD; sometimes we select a shorter sequence within the scene. In either case, scene analysis parallels the kind of textual analysis we frequently ask students to complete.

■■■■■■■■■■■■■■■■■

Film Analysis Activity III
Write about the scene you viewed by analyzing the following elements:

Plot: Write a short synopsis of the selected scene. What happens at the beginning, at the middle, and at the end of the scene?

Point of View: From whose point of view is the scene presented? How does the point of view affect a viewer's understanding of the scene? How does the camera clarify the point of view (types of shots, camera angles, duration of shots, etc.)?

Character: What is revealed about the characters in the scene and about their relationships with one another? How do movement, language, and costume contribute to an understanding of character?

Tone: What is the mood of the scene? How is the mood established? How do lighting, music, and camera technique contribute to an understanding of the mood?

Answer these questions individually or in groups. Share your observations with the class. Take viewing notes about the film clip/scene and develop these notes into an analytical essay about the scene.

■ ■ ■ ■ ■ ■ ■ ■ ■ ■ ■ ■ ■ ■ ■ ■ ■

Film as Text: Whole Film Analysis

To help students become active viewers, we like to have them practice viewer-response strategies. We encourage students to take notes on the film by providing them with a note-taking chart that they can fill in as they watch. Although many are reluctant to take notes, we insist. We hear complaints that note taking interrupts their viewing and that they sometimes get so caught up in the film that they forget to take notes, but we remain firm that notes enable all students to participate in the follow-up discussions and give them details and information to use as support when they write about film.

In addition to the sample note-taking guide provided in Figure 5.1, we always view films in segments, stopping periodically to discuss what students have noticed and to give them additional time to add their classmates' comments and observations to their note-taking charts. We encourage them to observe all elements of the film—the cinematic details, the literary details, and the dramatic details. (For more on these elements, see Teasley and Wilder.)

When students respond to the following questions *before* viewing the film, they prepare for the viewing experience. When students activate their prior knowledge, they start making predictions about the film they are about to see.

Previewing Questions

1. What is voice-over? Predict how you think this technique will be used in the film.

2. In some of the scenes, Chinese is spoken and English subtitles are provided. Why do you think the filmmakers used this strategy?

3. The sequence of stories in the film is different from the sequence that Tan uses in the book. Why would the film version require some adjustments to the order of the stories?

4. Some of the stories from the book are not included in the film. Why do you think the filmmakers omitted some stories? Which stories do you think might not transfer to film effectively? Why?

We designed the note-taking chart in Figure 5.1 to guide students *during* viewing. The chart helps them to record (and remember) their observations and contribute to a discussion about the film. In advance, we select stopping points, typically the end of a scene, at which we will ask students to share their ideas about the film from their note-taking charts (and add the ideas of others to their own charts). Discussion is usually lively and productive.

Note-Taking Chart for *The Joy Luck Club*

For each scene in the film, take notes on visual images, sound details, characters, objects, ANYTHING significant that you notice as you watch the scene. Use short phrases or abbreviations to assist you in taking notes.

Scene 1: Opening Titles/Hopes and Dreams

Scene 2: Auntie Lindo's Story

Scene 3: Waverly's Story

Scene 4: Auntie Ying-ying's Story

Scene 5: Lena's Story

Scene 6: Auntie An-mei's Story

Scene 7: Rose's Story

Scene 8: Auntie An-mei Continues

Scene 9: June's Story

Scene 10: Suyuan's Cherished Wish/End Credits

Figure 5.1

Finally, *after* the class has viewed the entire film, the following questions can be used to encourage class discussion. Any of these questions also can be assigned as a summative writing assignment once students have completed viewing the clips.

Postviewing Questions

1. How do the filmmakers transition from scene to scene? Is this an effective technique? Why or why not?

2. Discuss the use of particular objects in the film. What impact do these objects have on the characters and their development?

3. How does the film explore intergenerational conflict? How does the film explore generational conflict?

4. How do the images of China differ from the images of the United States in this film? How does the film explore these differences?

5. Although the film is based on a book, some of the scenes are without words. Discuss a scene without words. How does the camera make this scene effective?

6. Reconsider your predictions about the technique of voice-over and the use of subtitles. How effective were these strategies? Explain your reasoning.

7. How does the film develop the distinctions between the child (often told in flashback) and the adult that child became? What lesson is learned in the film? Who learns it? How?

The Book and the Movie: From Text to Film and Back Again

Instead of initiating a general discussion that compares and contrasts the book with the movie, we like to focus on a particular story and scene, at least initially. This activity requires a number of days to complete. In addition to reading excerpts from the book ("Two Kinds") and from Tan's nonfiction ("*Joy Luck* and Hollywood"), students hone their skills as future filmmakers and members of a group. As they consider the "filmable" moment in the story, they need to use their critical thinking skills to decide on the most effective section to film. In completing the storyboard chart (below), students activate their knowledge of film elements and film vocabulary. Finally, after viewing the actual film version of the story, students have the opportunity to practice comparing and contrasting their own conceptions of the scene with the film itself.

■■■■■■■■■■■■■■■■■

Writing Assignment:
From Text to Film and Back Again

Many films owe their lives to a work of literature. How could Clark Gable as Rhett Butler ever have uttered the most famous line in *Gone with the Wind* without the words of Margaret Mitchell's novel? And there are many other film-literature connections. Here's your opportunity to take text to film and back again.

1. Read the excerpt "Two Kinds" from *The Joy Luck Club* by Amy Tan (about Jing-mei Woo). This is your copy of the text, and as the future filmmaker it would be an excellent idea to highlight, annotate, color-code, and otherwise mark up this text. As you read, think about a section (not too long) of this text that you think is "filmable." Focus your notes on this section. Bring your text, notes, and ideas to class TOMORROW.

2. Work in small groups in class. First, share your ideas about the story. Then come to some agreement as to the best section of the story to make into a film. Talk about the scenes, shots, sequences, and details you would use. When you feel you've reached some consensus, develop a storyboard (see attached). Remember, this is a collaborative effort, so your work should reflect the ideas of the group members. Be ready to share your storyboard ideas with the rest of the class.

3. As background, please read an excerpt from Amy Tan's essay "*Joy Luck* and Hollywood" about her experiences transforming text into film.

4. Present your storyboards to the class. After each presentation, we'll have a brief critique and discussion of each group's ideas.

5. NOW, watch a clip from the film version of *The Joy Luck Club*. After viewing this film excerpt, write a well-developed paragraph in which you compare and contrast your group's storyboard to the actual film. What did Amy Tan and her co-writers do with this scene that you didn't do? What did you do that Amy Tan didn't do? Which approach do you think was more effective? Why?

Storyboard for *Joy Luck Club* ("Two Kinds")

You should have AT LEAST ten shots in your scene.

Refer to your film vocabulary glossary.

SCENE:_____

---

continued on next page

Shot Number	Visual Image	Characters and Objects	Camera Angles/ Movement	Sounds/ Music	Other Elements

Adapted from Pacesetter English (College Board Publications).

At the end of this activity, Eric Marman, an eleventh grader, wrote the following paragraphs comparing his imagined film version of "Two Kinds" and scene 1 of the actual film.

The difference between a book and a movie is that when you read a book, your interpretation could be completely different than what the author intended. With a movie, the audience sees exactly what the author of the screenplay intended for them to see. That's what makes Amy Tan's The Joy Luck Club so unique. The movie was made by the author herself. So every scene, every cut, every facial expression, every directing technique, was what the author was hoping a reader would imagine when reading her book. Therefore, the closer I was to creating the same storyboard as Tan, the better she did at describing her story in the novel.

The piano scene in the book version of <u>The Joy Luck Club</u> emphasizes the Ed Sullivan show and how her mother thought of the idea of having her daughter play piano. Since this was emphasized, I assumed that Tan would include it in her film. Instead, she skips immediately to the actual piano lessons, and uses a voice over to explain her mother's feelings and actions.

Also in the book, Tan goes directly from the talent show fiasco into her being an adult and being offered the piano by her mother. Naturally, as a reader, I predicted the movie would include a flash-forward where the character and her mom are talking about the piano. Tan obviously felt this part was not quite as important, and only hinted at it when she has one of her mother's friends ask the character why she does not take the piano home.

In the novel, Tan has the mother and father and aunt and uncle talking about the recital and the mother's disappointment is shown. When creating my film shot, I had the characters get on a bus, with a voice over of June speaking to describe what she was feeling. I felt this would incorporate as much of the book as possible. Tan didn't find this as important as I did and showed the mother's reaction purely through the facial expression. There was no bus, and there was no voice over until the next scene.

In truth, it is not my place to tell Amy Tan how to design the screenplay for her own book. What is so great about having the author design the screenplay is it gives the viewer an image of what he/she read in the book. Parts that I interpreted as important in the book were not even existent in the move. That's why Amy Tan's storyboard and my storyboard were so different, even after reading the same text.

—*Eric Marman*

Eric's response to viewing the film, after completing the two reading selections, the group discussion, and the storyboard activity, shows his appreciation for the decisions made by Tan and the director. He explains his reasoning behind the sequence of shots he would have made, but he also recognizes the bonus of having the author of the book as one of the screenwriters for the movie.

One Final Recommendation

As a final recommendation, we'd like to suggest looking at an excellent film study guide that is posted on Web English Teacher (under Literature/Prose/Amy Tan; see www.metromagazine.com.au/metro/studyguides/files/The_Joy_Luck_Club.pdf). Created by the Australian Teachers of Media Inc., the study guide includes an introduction, an exploration of some of the themes in the film, reactions to the film, an investigation of the characters in the film, an examination of the structure of the film, and a section titled "Responding to the Film's Text" that includes many thoughtful and challenging questions. Writing assignments, both tasks that respond to the text and personal writing, are also included.

To develop an effective list of key terms for film discussion (e.g., types of camera shots and angles, editing, sound), we recommend *Reel Conversations* (Teasley and Wilder) and www.riverhill.org/english/robb/documents/filmvocab.htm.

Scenic Overview of The Joy Luck Club the Film

The DVD version of the film identifies ten scene selections.

Scene 1: Opening Titles/Hopes and Dreams (First Prologue, "The Joy Luck Club" and "Two Kinds")

This brief scene begins impressionistically with muted grays, black, and white, visual images of the swan feather (the mother's good intentions) that is represented in the first prologue of the book. The prologue is read as a voice-over.

The scene then segues to a noisy party (this is the scene in which Amy Tan appears), and the main characters—three mothers, three daughters, and June—are introduced. The Aunties (Lindo, An-mei, and Ying-ying) and June begin their mahjong game, and June's voice-over explains the Joy Luck Club, the Aunties' connections to one another, and their worries about their own daughters.

The scene continues as June approaches the piano. As she plunks the keys, she flashes back to her childhood experiences playing the piano. She remembers (again through voice-over) her deaf piano teacher, her mother's competition with Auntie Lindo over their daughters' talents, her disastrous recital, and her confrontation with her mother after the recital. The scene then segues to June's mother's story, the tale of her journey, her illness, and the loss of her twin daughters. The scene transitions to a church picnic in the present time where the Aunties reveal that they have found the lost babies, now grown women, and that June is invited to China to meet her sisters.

The scene then switches to the mahjong game, and the Aunties reveal that they have not told June the truth about her visit to China: they have not told the lost daughters that their mother is dead. This revelation leads Lindo to flash back on her own experience with her mother when she gave her up as a child.

Scene 2: Auntie Lindo's Story ("The Red Candle")

This scene, in Chinese with English subtitles, depicts Lindo's arranged marriage at the age of four. Lindo relates through voice-over her separation from her mother, her marriage ceremony, and her stormy marriage with her immature husband. When her mother-in-law berates her for not conceiving, Lindo develops an elaborate plan to escape from her marriage. The scene segues to the present and Lindo's daughter Waverly.

Scene 3: Waverly's Story ("Four Directions" and "Double Face")

This scene begins in a beauty shop in the present time where Waverly is arranging a makeover for her mother. Waverly flashes back to her childhood and her time as a chess prodigy and champion. Embarrassed by her mother's bragging, Waverly refuses to continue to play chess. When she does try to return to the game, she is unsuccessful and vows never to play again. Waverly recalls her unsuccessful first marriage and her current American boyfriend's disastrous mistakes during a meal her mother prepares. The scene ends by returning to present time and, through an effective use of mirror images at the beauty parlor, Waverly and Lindo come to terms with each other. A short scene at a going-away party for June concludes scene 3 and connects to scene 4.

Scene 4: Auntie Ying-ying's Story ("Waiting between the Trees")

In this flashback scene, Ying-ying at the age of sixteen falls in love with and marries a man who turns out to be cruel, abusing her both verbally and physically. This flashback contains a scene in which Ying-ying undresses and also a sexually explicit scene. Eventually, in a scene reminiscent of *Medea*, Ying-ying takes from her husband the one thing that would matter, his son. At the conclusion of the scene, Ying-ying moves to the United States, remarries, and has a daughter, Lena, but Ying-ying has "no spirit" to give her.

Scene 5: Lena's Story ("Rice Husband")

The scene begins with an effective overhead shot of Lena and Ying-ying walking up the spiral staircase of Lena's modern and spartan home. Lena and her husband have a "50-50 relationship" in which they share all expenditures. While Ying-ying settles into the guest room (filmed in stark gray sterility), Lena confronts her husband and reflects on their loveless marriage. (Feminine products are mentioned in the conversation.) As Lena faces the impending end of her marriage, Ying-ying tips over a table and breaks a vase. Lena goes to her mother's room and, in a voice-over, Ying-ying asserts that her daughter will hear her and that she will give her the courage to leave.

The scene concludes with a return to June's party and a conversation between the daughters. June, telling the story of the swan feather to a young child as she puts her down for a nap, explains the good intentions that all mothers have for their children.

Scene 6: Auntie An-mei's Story ("Scar")
In this scene (in Chinese with English subtitles), An-mei remembers her own childhood and her mother's shame. As An-mei's grandmother lies ill, An-mei's mother returns home and, in a ritualistic scene, cuts off a portion of her own flesh to make a soup for her ailing mother, as a dutiful daughter should do to save her mother's life. As An-mei's mother prepares to leave again, An-mei decides to leave with her. The scene returns to the present as An-mei meets her daughter Rose at a grocery story where Rose is purchasing supplies to make a cake for her husband. An-mei questions Rose's intentions.

Scene 7: Rose's Story ("Half and Half")
Rose reflects on her romance and marriage to Ted, an American man, and his family's racist view of her Chinese heritage. Rose loses herself in her husband's life, attempting to please and serve him. After the birth of their child, their marriage breaks up and Ted asks Rose to sell the house. At the end of the scene, An-mei in

the present discusses her concern that Rose is begging Ted to pay attention to her and that Rose, like An-mei's mother, does not know her own worth. This scene contains a number of expletives.

Scene 8: Auntie An-mei's Story Continues ("Magpies")

An-mei continues the story of her mother's tragic life by telling of her new family, Wu Tsing and his four wives and their children. She flashes back to Wu Tsing's rape of her mother. Her mother, pregnant and disowned, has no choice but to go to Wu Tsing's house. After the birth of An-mei's son, Second Wife claims the child as her reward for bringing An-mei's mother to Wu Tsing. An-mei's mother eventually commits suicide, and at her funeral An-mei "learns to shout." She warns Wu Tsing and Second Wife that her mother's ghost will haunt them for their cruelties.

The scene then segues to Rose, who is waiting in the rain outside her house for her husband's arrival. Rose asserts herself when she tells her husband that she will not sell the house, nor will she give up their daughter.

A final short section of the scene returns to the party, where everyone is remembering dinners and feasts of the past. Lindo serves the famous crab dish that June's mother once prepared.

Scene 9: June's Story ("Best Quality")

June remembers a dinner with herself and her mother and Waverly and Auntie Lindo. During the meal, Waverly insults June's work as a copywriter and humiliates June in front of her family. Later, as June and her mother are cleaning up from the meal, June suggests to her mother that she must wish for a better daughter than June is. June's mother responds by giving June her jade necklace and commenting on June's "best-quality heart."

The scene ends by returning again to the party. The guests have all departed and June is cleaning up when she encounters Auntie Lindo in the dining room. Lindo confesses that she has not told June the truth about her impending trip to China. She admits that June's long-lost sisters do not know of their mother's death and that June will have to tell them when she arrives. As June finishes packing, her father gives her some photographs of her mother to give to her sisters.

Scene 10: Suyuan's Cherished Wish/End Credits ("A Pair of Tickets")

The final scene of the film returns to the opening scene, in which June's mother abandons her babies. In a voice-over, June explains that her mother survived but was never able to find her daughters. June recalls the gift of the swan feather and thinks about what she will tell her sisters about her mother when they meet. When June arrives in China, she sees her sisters, tells them of her mother's death, and reveals that she "has come to take her place."

The final images in the movie are of two still pictures. One photograph captures all four mothers and daughters. The final photograph shows June, without her mother, posing with her three Aunties and their daughters.

6 Taking a Critical Stance: Argument and Assessment

■ ■

Much criticism of *The Joy Luck Club* exists in literary journals, on the Internet, and even in books. Although students can profit from reading and analyzing some of it, we believe that a sound way to approach criticism is to involve students in the same debates and disagreements the critics themselves engage in. Furthermore, developing an argument about either an issue within the book or one that uses the book as evidence and support is good practice for the standardized tests students face today, especially the SAT essay and, for some, the Advanced Placement exam, as well as preparation for college-level writing.

Students have found the template in Figure 6.1 very helpful because it gives them a step-by-step method for analyzing an argument and then developing their own position in response. Admittedly, this template is somewhat prescriptive, but it provides students with a process they can internalize and use—and modify, adapt, and enhance—as they develop more sophisticated skills with argumentative strategies. It also has the advantage of discouraging the "three reasons" argument that leads to a five-paragraph essay without any consideration of counterargument. Furthermore, the template format requires students to quote directly from the argument they are reading, so it's really a note-

---

Argument Template

The general argument made by author X in her/his work,

_____, is that _____. More specifically,

X argues that _____. She/He

writes, "_____

_____." In this passage, X is suggesting that

_____. In conclusion, X's belief

is that _____

_____.

   In my view, X is wrong/right because _____. More

specifically, I believe that _____. For

example, _____. Although X

might object that _____, I maintain that

_____. Therefore, I conclude

that _____.

(From *Clueless in Academe* by Gerald Graff, Yale UP 2003, pp. 169–70.)

Figure 6.1

taking device as well. With this template as an outline of sorts,
students are ready to write fairly fleshed out arguments of their
own.

   With a sound grasp of argument and *The Joy Luck Club* itself,
students are ready to examine criticism of both book and film.
Following are excerpts interpreting the book and the film that
invite students to take an argumentative stance.

Masking: An Interpretation

Critic Ben Xu argues that Lindo Jong wears a mask, what he calls "an heroic act," and develops an interpretation of her as having a "victim mentality":

> The wearing of a mask is to Lindo Jong an heroic act—an act necessary for the survival of poor immigrants like herself, who feel "it's hard to keep your Chinese face in America" (294). Wearing a mask means the ability to suppress one's true feelings and emotions—even to deceive—in order to be allowed to live. She is not unaware of the debt that the mask wearer has to pay to human guile; but in her understanding there is no rage that rips the heart, no passion of combat which stresses the heroic deeds of ethnic rebellion. With many Chinese-Americans like Lindo Jong, survivalism has led to a cynical devaluation of heroism, and to a resignation that is tinged with a bitter sense of humor.
>
> When they first arrived in America, Lindo Jong and An-mei Hsu worked in a fortune cookie factory, making Chinese sayings of fortune for American consumption. Lindo Jong was wondering what all this nonsense of Chinese fortunes was about. An-mei explained to her:

> > "American people think Chinese people write these sayings."
> >
> > "But we never say such things!" [Lindo Jong] said. "These things don't make sense. These are not fortunes, they are bad instructions."
> >
> > "No, miss," [An-Mei] said, laughing, "it is our bad fortune to be here making these and somebody else's bad fortune to pay to get them."

Lindo Jong knows that the Chinese wearing of the mask, just like these Chinese fortunes, can convince many Americans that they know and understand Chinese people. She also has an unusual insight into the risk that the mask wearer can become psychologically dependent upon the mask, even when the mask is not needed. Continued wearing of the mask makes it difficult for the wearer of the mask to be her real self. Maskedness has almost become the ethnic symbolism for Chinese-Americans like Lindo Jong, who thinks like a person of "two faces," being neither American nor Chinese. (304)

In a self-consciously two-faced person like Lindo Jong we find a detached, bemused, ironic observer who is almost fascinated by the fact that she has not a self that she can claim as "me." The sense of being an observer of one's own situation and that all things are not happening to "me" helps to protect "me" against pain and also to control expressions of outrage or rebellion. Survivors have to learn to see themselves not as free subjects, but rather as the victims of circumstances, be they the current situation or prefixed fate of disposition. (Xu 11)

Source: Ben Xu. "Memory and the Ethnic Self: Reading Amy Tan's *The Joy Luck Club*. *MELUS* 19.4 (Spring 1994): 3–18.

Students might discuss or write about this idea of masking as it applies to mothers and daughters in *The Joy Luck Club* or in comparison with other works of literature by writers of color, women writers, immigrants, or anyone who feels marginalized.

▪ ▪ ▪ ▪ ▪ ▪ ▪ ▪ ▪ ▪ ▪ ▪ ▪ ▪ ▪ ▪ ▪ ▪

> ### Writing Assignment
> Do you wear a mask? When? Where? Why? Is the mask self-imposed or forced on you? Is there a temptation to become "psychologically dependent" on the mask? You might consider other literary works that offer themselves as intriguing companions to explore this concept, including "We Wear the Mask" by Paul Laurence Dunbar, *The Catcher in the Rye* by J. D. Salinger, and "Shooting an Elephant" by George Orwell.

▪ ▪ ▪ ▪ ▪ ▪ ▪ ▪ ▪ ▪ ▪ ▪ ▪ ▪ ▪ ▪ ▪ ▪

Failed Waverly: An Interpretation

Another character who has turned out to be fairly controversial among critics is Waverly. In a critical essay on "Rules of the Game," David Kelly argues that "readers who interpret this story as the tale of Waverly's learning life's rules are missing an important part of it." Since this mother-daughter story is so crucial to *The Joy Luck Club*, a close analysis of this critic's reasoning leads to provocative discussions and potentially powerful argumentative essays. Kelly also makes assertions about children of immigrants and Tan's use of the chess metaphor that are integral to the logic of his argument and, thus, important to deal with in any response.

> This, in the end, is a curse that both children of immigrants and all adolescents share: they outgrow their parents. First-generation Americans find themselves better able to function in society than their parents are, owing to the fact that they are in a world they have known most of their lives. Similarly, adolescents are destined to eventually reach the

age when they recognize that they are self-sufficient humans, able to survive outside of their parents' control. The same social dynamic that is at work in both cases would also apply to the case of a famous child like the story's chess prodigy, whose parents are ordinary people. All three situations lead to frustrated rebellion: unlike the rebellion of children who break away from the hold of dominating parents, rebellion is not satisfying for those who simply outgrow their parents. Part of the reason for this is that such rebellion is just too easy. The fact that Waverly ends this story so abruptly, contemplating her next move like a chess player, seems to be Tan's admission that she has her character in a situation that has no easy solution, one which may, in fact, have no solution at all. Waverly is bound by love to her mother, but her mother has made her grow up too fast to cope with the social elements that are destined to force her in new directions.

Games are always a reflection of life with the main difference being that their rules are laid out in advance, instead of being discovered. The distinction is crucial: it is the reason that most comparisons between life and games fail when given serious scrutiny. Of all games, chess is probably the one most often used in literature to symbolize life's strategies, if for no other reason than that it has existed in cultures around the globe for fifteen centuries. In "Rules of the Game" Waverly Jong, being just a child, takes the relationship between chess and life too seriously, mainly because the rule her mother gave her about "invisible strength" gives her nearly supernatural power in competition. She fails to see the difference between the game and real life, and as a result finds that life is grander but less manageable than she thinks it should be. Her frustration is natural—it comes from being a child, particularly the child of an immigrant family—but it is made all the worse when circumstances force her to grow up too fast. Readers who interpret this story as the tale of Waverly learning life's rules are missing an important part of it: the point of the story is that there are no rules that cover all of life's possibilities.

Source: David Kelly. Critical essay on "Rules of the Game." *Short Stories for Students*, Vol. 16. Detroit: Gale Group, 2003.

Writing Assignment

Select one of the following statements and explain why you agree or disagree:

- ■ "All adolescents share" the "curse" of "outgrow[ing] their parents."
- ■ "First-generation Americans find themselves better able to function in society than their [immigrant] parents."
- ■ "Rebellion is not satisfying for those who simply outgrow their parents."
- ■ Waverly's mother made her "grow up too fast to cope with the social elements that are destined to force her in new directions."
- ■ "Games are always a reflection of life."
- ■ Waverly "fails to see the difference between the [chess] game and real life."

Each one of these statements points to a premise in Kelly's logic and underscores the complexity of responding to an argument in the fullness of its claims, assumptions, and evidence rather than simply to the main point. In other words, students have to examine the construction of someone else's argument before they can write their own.

The Ending

Some have criticized the ending of *The Joy Luck Club*, asserting that having Suyuan's daughters reunited with one another and the spirit of their dead mother oversimplifies a complex and problematic relationship. In his dissertation, Stephen Souris was one of these critics, though in subsequent writings he recanted and gave the ending a more sympathetic reading. Students might write their own arguments by agreeing or disagreeing with the position Souris originally held.

> The reader's sense of the poignancy inherent in a situation where mothers and daughters do not communicate as fully as they might in itself implies a remedy, in itself motivates the reader to imagine a solution—one that would accommodate the needs of both mothers and daughters. . . . *The Joy Luck Club* interferes with the imagined affirmation by prodding the reader too much. It is one thing to show Waverly, at the close of "Four Directions," attempting to impose an artificial, superficial pleasantness on her deeply problematic relationship with her mother by thinking about taking her mother with her on her honeymoon: that reveals an interesting split within this particular consciousness; it is another matter to have Tan [impose] a superficial sense of

harmony at the end of the book that does not do justice to the actual diversity and conflict between the covers. The collection of stories is full of moral potential without the heavy-handed ending simply through its presentation of multiple voices, artistically organized. (284–85)

Source: Stephen Souris. "Recent American Multiple Narrator Novels: A Bakhtinian/Iserian Analysis." Diss. University of Wisconsin–Madison, 1992. See also Stephen Souris, "'Only Two Kinds of Daughters': Inter-Monologue Dialogicity in *The Joy Luck Club*." *MELIS* 19.2 (Summer 1994): 99–123.

Even a short excerpt such as this one can serve as a viable prompt for students to construct a basic argument by, initially, taking the quote into account and, then, developing their own position either in support of or as a challenge to the opinion expressed in the quote. Approaching argument this way also encourages students to understand the concept of counterargument because they must explain and respond to a position different from their own. If they disagree with the quote, it can stand as the counterargument. If they agree with it, they must formulate on their own the opposing position.

Writing Assignment

Write an essay in which you support, refute, or qualify Souris's position that the ending of *The Joy Luck Club* is unsatisfactory.

Assessment: SAT and Advanced Placement (AP) English

The types of discussions and writings we discuss in this chapter
encourage students to engage in critical thinking that takes the
form of argument, both arguments that are interpretations of literature and ones that take a position on an issue related to the
literature.

In 2005 the College Board, creators of the SAT college-en-
trance exam, added to the test a required essay component, a
twenty-five-minute task in which students must construct an argument. In some instances, students are given quotations to which
they respond; there may be one quotation or two conflicting ones.
In others, they are simply asked an argumentative question. Following are simulated SAT-type questions that we created for students to use with *The Joy Luck Club* as evidence in their response.
(Of course, actual SAT essay topics do not require reference to
any specific text.)

■ Is full assimilation desirable or even possible? When people come
from one country or culture to another, many want to assimilate
into their new home as fully as possible, while others prefer to
retain many of their native customs and traditions. Which do you
believe is the better choice in order to succeed in an adopted
homeland? Support your response with *The Joy Luck Club* as well
as your own experience and observations.

■ Marian Wright Edelman, founder of the Children's Defense Fund,
has stated: "In reality, no parent raises a child alone." Many would
claim that the problems of youth today would be solved if more
people believed as Edelman does. Write an essay supporting or
challenging the idea that child rearing should not be the exclu-

sive responsibility of a parent or parents. Support your response with *The Joy Luck Club* as well as your own experience and observations.

- In her essay "Required Reading and Other Dangerous Subjects," Amy Tan writes, "I am an American writer. I am Chinese by racial heritage. I am Chinese-American by family and social upbringing. . . . My characters may be largely Chinese-American, but I think Chinese-Americans are part of America." Write an essay in which you agree or disagree with Amy Tan's position by focusing on whether you believe *The Joy Luck Club* is part of mainstream American literature.

- Are high expectations a prerequisite for success or a recipe for failure? Sometimes a teacher's or parent's high expectations can encourage a child; in other instances, the pressure of such expectations may bring about failure or disappointment. Do you agree or disagree? Take a position and present a cogent argument using *The Joy Luck Club*, other examples from literature, and your own experience or that of your peers as support.

In the so-called open question on the AP English Literature Exam, students are given a specific interpretive lens and asked to apply it to a literary work. Each year a list of works (plays and novels) appears as part of the question, and students are invited to choose from that list or select another work "of comparable literary merit." Following are four past questions that seem particularly applicable to *The Joy Luck Club*. (The suggested time for answering these questions is forty minutes.)

- Some works of literature use the element of time in a distinct way. The chronological sequence of events may be altered, or time may be suspended or accelerated. Choose a novel, an epic, or a play of recognized literary merit and show how the author's manipulation of time contributes to the effectiveness of the work as a whole. (1986)

- Many plays and novels use contrasting places (for example, two countries, two cities or towns, two houses, or the land and the sea) to represent opposed forces or ideas that are central to the meaning of the work. Choose a novel or a play that contrasts two such places. Write an essay explaining how the places differ, what each place represents, and how their contrast contributes to the meaning of the work. (1991)

- In some works of literature, a character who appears briefly, or does not appear at all, is a significant presence. Choose a novel or play of literary merit and write an essay in which you show how such a character functions in the work. You may wish to discuss how the character affects action, theme, or the development of other characters. (1994)

- Critic Roland Barthes has said, "Literature is the question minus the answer." Choose a novel or play and, considering Barthes' observation, write an essay in which you analyze a central question the work raises and the extent to which it offers any answers. Explain how the author's treatment of this question affects your understanding of the work as a whole. (2004)

▪ ▪ ▪ ▪ ▪ ▪ ▪ ▪ ▪ ▪ ▪ ▪ ▪ ▪ ▪ ▪ ▪

The AP essays are evaluated holistically on a scale of 1 to 9. For more information (including sample questions, scoring guides, and student responses), go to the official Web site, AP Central (http://apcentral.collegeboard.com).

We know from various assessments at the state and national levels that writing argument is extremely difficult for most students, a point that the change in the SAT to include a required argumentative question underscores. We've suggested a few approaches to teaching argument in the discussions thus far in this chapter, but these AP and SAT-type questions are an opportunity to explore even more concrete strategies.

Film Review as Argument

Argument exists in varied forms, and reviews—of books, films, concerts, plays, CDs—are familiar to students, easily accessible, and topical. Asking students to agree or disagree with one of the following reviews of *The Joy Luck Club* increases their critical thinking about the film and gives them yet another opportunity to practice argumentative writing.

Each of the reviews addresses a different element of the film. Howe argues that its strength lies in its honest depiction of character and its avoidance of Asian stereotypes. Leong compliments Wang's direction and the strengths of the stories themselves, but he criticizes the dialogue and language in the modern-day scenes as being stilted. Finally, Bernardinelli suggests that the film slips into melodrama and, in the process, manipulates the emotions of the viewer.

I. Director Wayne Wang is not a streamlined, cut-to-the-quick kind of director. His style is respectful, if not plodding. He's pointed helpfully in the right direction by a sturdy—if overly deliberate—framework created by screenwriter Ronald Bass and Tan. In a drama of multiple plot lines, the movie makes clear and vivid sense. And, in addition to its storytelling wealth, *Joy Luck Club* is nourishing for its avoidance of Asian stereotypes. There isn't the slightest trace of a laundry man, kung fu killer, or aphorism-spouting, pidgin-English-speaking detective. This mah-jong epic is far too busy with original human entanglements to pay attention to such tired figures of Hollywood yesteryear.

Source: Desson Howe, 1993. Film review of *The Joy Luck Club. The Washington Post* (September 24) <http://www.washington post.com/wp-srv/style/longterm/movies/videos/thejoyluck clubrhowe_a0aff7.htm>.

II. The only criticism that can be leveled against *The Joy Luck Club* is the wavering quality of the acting and the scripted dialogue. At times, particularly in the scenes that take place in the modern day, the film seems to stumble with pretentious-sounding line delivery and overly flowery conversation. Thankfully, there is an underlying earnestness to the story, and coupled with Wang's skillful direction, these transgressions are forgivable.

Source: Anthony Leong, 2002. Film review of *The Joy Luck Club.*
Media Circus.net (January 24) <http://www.embanet.com/entertain-ment/_disc8/000000cd.htm>.

▪ ▪ ▪ ▪ ▪ ▪ ▪ ▪ ▪ ▪ ▪ ▪ ▪ ▪ ▪ ▪

III. *The Joy Luck Club* is clearly—perhaps too clearly—an adaptation of a book. The dialogue is often too poetic to be real, and the story too clearly plotted to be acceptable as anything more than an imperfect reflection of the world we live in. The line between drama and melodrama is a fine one, and, while *The Joy Luck Club* most often successfully navigates the tightrope, there are times when it slips and comes across as heavy-handed. This film is no stranger to moments of manipulation.

Source: James Bernardinelli, 1993. Film review of *The Joy Luck Club*. *Colossus.net* <http://movie-reviews.colossus.net/movies/j/joy_luck.html>.

▪ ▪ ▪ ▪ ▪ ▪ ▪ ▪ ▪ ▪ ▪ ▪ ▪ ▪ ▪ ▪

Writing Assignment

After reading the excerpts from the reviews, select one review to use as the basis for an argumentative essay. Write a multiparagraph argumentative response. Select one of the following position statements and then use notes and your understanding of the film as supportive evidence. (See argument template.)

Statement 1—I agree (or disagree) with reviewer Desson Howe that the film version of *The Joy Luck Club* avoids stereotyping Asian characters.

Statement 2–I agree (or disagree) with reviewer Anthony Leong that the dialogue in the modern-day scenes in the film version of *The Joy Luck Club* sounds pretentious and too flowery.

Statement 3–I agree (or disagree) with reviewer James Bernardinelli that the film version of *The Joy Luck Club* is melodramatic and manipulates the emotions of the viewer.

Taking a position on film criticism requires a great deal of thinking on students' part. They must, for example, think not just about what they've noticed about this film but also often about what they know about other films. In reflecting on stereotypes, students will need to think about the ways that other films have presented Asian characters. Some may be familiar with the Chinese detective Charlie Chan or the martial arts wizard Jackie Chan or even the artful swordplay and mysticism of films like *Crouching Tiger, Hidden Dragon* or *House of Flying Daggers*. Students need to reflect on the dialogue in the film and consider what authentic speech really is. And students will need to consider whether the film has in any way manipulated their emotions. Whichever pathway students take with this assignment, teachers can be sure that they are reflecting, thinking, and, once again, practicing their argumentative skills.

Writing Assignment

Write a film review of the film version of *The Joy Luck Club* using your notes.

1. Your introduction should include relevant background and general information about the film (director, actors, screenwriters, and other significant pieces of information).

2. Provide a brief summary or synopsis of the film. Remember that reviewers rarely give away the ending, so think about the kinds of things a viewer might need to know if he or she were going to decide whether to see this movie. Try to limit your summary to five to six sentences (approximately).

3. Analyze some particular aspect of the film. Think about the characters, plot, or themes. Reflect on dialogue, acting, sets, or costumes. Focus on cinematic elements such as editing (cuts), sound, visual effects, or camera angles. In this section of your review, you should focus on a specific sequence of shots in the film. Do not try to cover the entire film. This is the section of your review where you analyze a highlight or low point.

4. Conclude your review by offering a summative evaluation and recommendation. Would you recommend this film? For what kind of audience?

7 Connections and Extensions

As English teachers, we face the challenge of "making new friends but keeping the old" when it comes to integrating new texts into the curriculum. We worry about what we might have to forfeit in order to add new works. The trick, if that's the word, is finding connections so that the work of more contemporary authors such as Amy Tan fits in thematically or pairs as a companion with other texts already part of our classroom and as a link to other disciplines. Such connections are hardly necessary to justify including Tan, who is widely enough recognized on her own merits, but they enrich both the new works and the more tried-and-true. Making these connections is good synergy.

Connecting with the Canon—and Beyond

Many mainstream literary texts commonly taught in the English classroom connect to the ideas explored in *The Joy Luck Club* and serve as wonderful companions and counterpoints to Tan's book. To explore intergenerational differences, for example, consider pairing *The Joy Luck Club* with Shakespeare's *King Lear*, *To Kill a Mockingbird* by Harper Lee, or *Death of a Salesman* by Arthur Miller. Have students reflect on the similarities and differences of parent-child relationships. Are these significant differences? Is conflict a natural result of intergenerational relationships? Do mothers have different expectations for their children than fathers do?

Another pairing that we've found effective is comparing a traditional, small-town American experience with an immigrant experience—*Our Town* by Thornton Wilder and *The Joy Luck Club,* for example. Ask students to write about the differences between Emily Gibbs and her family and immigrant families chronicled in *The Joy Luck Club.* How does the small-town American experience differ from the immigrant Chinese experience?

More sophisticated student readers do well pairing texts with similar structures. Both William Faulkner's *As I Lay Dying* and Tan's *The Joy Luck Club* use multivoiced narratives. How do the writers create such unique voices? Are Faulkner and Tan equally successful?

There is certainly a kinship between the characters in *The Joy Luck Club* and those in books by other Asian American writers. Consider preparing comparative units or outside reading assignments that pair *The Joy Luck Club* with Maxine Hong Kingston's *The Woman Warrior*, Frank Chin's *Donald Duk*, Gish Jen's *Typical American*, Fae Myenne Ng's *Bone*, or Gus Lee's *China Boy*. Younger students enjoy an earlier work, the charming *Fifth Chinese Daughter* by Jade Snow Wong (who is the self-described *first* Asian American writer). Through Joy Kogawa's *Obasan* and Hisaye Yamamoto's *Seventeen Syllables and Other Stories*, students can explore the experience of Japanese mothers and their second-generation daughters before, during, and after World War II. Ask students to consider whether these writers share common themes, similar conflicts, and parallel experiences in their books.

Other works that have entered our classrooms through the efforts of multiculturalism work well with *The Joy Luck Club.* Sandra Cisneros's popular *The House on Mango Street* shares a similar structure of vignettes. Students might compare and contrast Esperanza's understanding of heritage and neighborhood with Waverly's or Jing-mei's appreciation of heritage and family. *Brown Girl, Brownstones* by Paule Marshall offers a look into a family that has emigrated from Barbados. How are the central character and Jing-mei similar?

Another interesting companion piece is James McBride's *The Color of Water*. Have students consider how McBride's relationship with his mother differs from and compares to the daughters' relationships with their mothers in *The Joy Luck Club*. How do the characters in both books face imbalance and find balance through their family relationships?

Connecting with Social Studies

Students who are studying modern world history bring a wealth of contextual understanding to *The Joy Luck Club* and classroom discussions. What were U.S. immigration policies for the Chinese? What was the War Bride Act of 1945? What is the Kuomintang? What role did the Chinese play in the building of U.S. railroads, and what is the derivation of the expression "Chinaman's chance"? From Chairman Mao's Cultural Revolution and his Little Red Book to the Tiananmen Square protests, students share and explore a background knowledge that deepens their understanding of *The Joy Luck Club*. We urge colleagues to form partnerships if at all possible with social studies teachers to develop activities that enrich both courses. A history teacher we know begins his Modern World History class every day with a quotation from Mao's Little Red Book (selected by students) and exercise.

An excellent resource on the Chinese immigration experience is the textbook *American Mosaic: Multicultural Readings in Context* by Barbara Roche Rico and Sandra Mano. Their chapter

"Chinese Immigrants: The Lure of the Gold Mountain" includes background on historical, literary, and cultural contexts; an excerpt from the Chinese Exclusion Act of 1882; an essay by Betty Lee Sung, "The Pioneer Chinese," which details the experiences of early Chinese immigrants; and some examples of the Gold Mountain poems. In addition to other readings, the chapter concludes with a series of critical thinking and writing questions (called "Connecting").

Given the predictions of the role China will play in the twenty-first century—when the students we have today will be taking charge—the more we can do to promote deeper awareness of the history, politics, culture, economics, and social contexts of China, the better. *The Joy Luck Club* could be one cog in that wheel of understanding and appreciation.

Connecting with Art

The Smithsonian Institution's Freer Gallery of Art has one of the best collections of Chinese art in this country. Their Web site contains visual images of paintings, sculptures, and carvings in their Chinese collections. Additional museum Web sites on Chinese art include the Cincinnati Art Museum; the Cleveland Museum of Art; the Chinese Art Gallery in San Leandro, California; and the Chinese Culture Center of San Francisco. Have students examine some of the examples of Chinese art on these Web sites and make their own connections to ideas and images presented in *The Joy Luck Club*. Lu Ch'ai, a painter during the seventeenth century, gives advice about the rules of painting. He recommends that one "see the great in the small" and "see the small in the perspective of the great." Do the mothers and daughters in Tan's book have this vision?

Making Connections with and through Language

It may sound traditional, but we believe that at some point just about every class should do some deliberate and focused explorations of language—of its power and possibilities. *The Joy Luck Club* offers easy avenues into such discussions because language is the stage for acting out cultural differences in this book. The opening fable about the swan describes the mother's dream of her daughter speaking "only perfect American English," and she waits for the time she can herself speak "in perfect American English" (17). All the daughters in the book understand Chinese, but they speak English; in contrast, the mothers speak a patois of Chinese and English that often confuses their daughters.

Ask students to note ways in which language becomes an instrument of political power. How do characters use language strategically? What realizations do they have about how fluency in English empowers them? Ying-ying, for example, refers derisively to her daughter's profession of being an architect as "arty-tecky" (242). When Suyuan is angry with her daughter for not applying herself to the piano, June hears her muttering "so ungrateful" in Chinese (136).

Tan stresses the difficulties, even impossibilities, of translation. June recognizes that there is no translation for *joy luck*: "They [the aunts] see that joy and luck do not mean the same to their daughters, that to these closed American-born minds 'joy luck' is not a word, it does not exist. They see daughters who will bear grandchildren born without any connecting hope from generation to generation" (40–41). In other instances, Tan incorporates Chinese expressions. After her mother has mocked her daughter's psychiatrist, Rose thinks, "And everything around me seemed to be *heimongmong*. These were words I had never thought about in

English terms. I suppose the closest in meaning would be 'confused' and 'dark fog'" (188).

Extending beyond the book itself, we have developed a mini–case study—a set of readings—on language, with Tan's excellent essay "Mother Tongue" as the centerpiece. This essay, originally published in the *Threepenny Review* in 1991, explains her growing awareness of "the different Englishes" she uses and includes several anecdotes about her mother, whom Tan at one point describes as speaking "impeccable broken English." Tan discusses the prejudice against those who speak English with an accent or in so-called nonstandard dialects, and in a moving conclusion, she explains why the reader she envisions for her work is her mother.

In this case study, we include a number of passages from fiction and nonfiction describing the language experiences of immigrants and other minorities. These pieces, along with "Mother Tongue" and *The Joy Luck Club*, invite a range of student writing:

Writing Assignments

■ Discuss ways in which language divides parents and children. How does language reverse the usual power relationship between parents and children? What is the relationship between power, language, and identity?

■ Analyze the types of prejudice against language differences. Are these prejudices you have seen in your own communities, perhaps even classrooms?

- Research the English-only legislation proposed by many states and adopted by some. Should yours become (or should it have become) an English-only state?

- Write your own literacy narratives that focus on experiences acquiring language or learning about the power inherent in language proficiency.

- Explore authors who write in English but use another language in their work without translating it (e.g., Cormac McCarthy's or Sandra Cisneros's use of Spanish, Edwidge Danticat's use of Haitian creole). What is the author's motivation? Is it the same as that of Zora Neale Hurston when she included dialect in *Their Eyes Were Watching God*?

- Consider the language of e-mail as a dialect. Are all e-mails alike, or does the audience influence the choices in the type of language the writer uses?

Our list of readings that pair well with "Mother Tongue" or *The Joy Luck Club* include the following:

- *The Winged Seed* by Li-Young Lee
- *Monkey Bridge* by Lan Cao
- "Aria: A Memoir of a Bilingual Childhood" by Richard Rodriguez
- "How to Tame a Wild Tongue" by Gloria Anzaldúa
- *Breath, Eyes, Memory* by Edwidge Danticat
- "Lullaby" by Leslie Marmon Silko

■■■■■■■■■■■■■■■■■

Writing Assignment

Both the essay "Mother Tongue" and the following passage from the novel *Monkey Bridge* by Vietnamese American writer Lan Cao explore the shift in power of the normal parent-child relationship as a result of language acquisition. Write an essay comparing and contrasting the experiences of the two daughters. Consider the attitude each has toward her mother.

My superior English meant that, unlike my mother and Mrs. Bay, I knew the difference between "cough" and "enough," "bough" and "through," "trough" and "thorough," "dough" and "fought." Once I made it past the fourth or fifth week in Connecticut, the new language Uncle Michael and Aunt Mary were teaching me began gathering momentum, like tumbleweed in a storm. This was my realization: we have only to let one thing go—the language we think in, or the composition of our dream, the grass roots clinging underneath its rocks—and all at once everything goes. It had astonished me, the ease with which continents shift and planets change course, the casual way in which the earth goes about shedding the laborious folds of its memories. Suddenly, out of that difficult space between here and there, English revealed itself to me with the ease of thread unspoiled. I began to understand the levity and weight of its sentences. First base, second base, home run. New terminologies were not difficult to master, and gradually the possibility of perfection began edging its way into my life. How did those numerous Chinatowns and Little Italys sustain the will to maintain a distance, the desire to inhabit the edge and margin of American life? A mere eight weeks into Farmington, and the American Dream was exerting a sly but seductive pull.

By the time I left Farmington to be with my mother, I had already created for myself a different, more sacred tongue. Khe Sanh, the Tet Offensive, the Ho Chi Minh Trail—a history as imperfect as my once obviously imperfect English—these were things that had rushed me into the American melting pot. And when I saw my mother again, I was no longer the same person she used to know. Inside my new tongue, my real tongue, was an astonishing new power. For my mother and her Vietnamese neighbors, I became the keeper of the word, the only one with access to the light world. Like Adam, I had the God-given right to name all the fowls of the air and all the beasts of the field. (36-37)

8 More . . .

■ ■

We've focused on two important works by Amy Tan, *The Joy Luck Club* and *The Opposite of Fate*. Tan has, however, written several novels and two children's books.

Other Works by Amy Tan

The Kitchen God's Wife (1991)

This is Tan's second book and also widely acclaimed (another bestseller). The story revolves around a mother (Jiang Weili/Winnie) and her daughter Pearl. Winnie reveals her escape from her disastrous first marriage (to a fighter pilot in the Sino-Japanese war) and that she is uncertain if he is Pearl's father. Pearl eventually finds the strength to confide her secret illness to her mother.

The Hundred Secret Senses (1995)

This novel chronicles a series of secrets told through memory and imagination. At age three, Olivia finds herself with a new, Chinese half sister, Kwan, who excites her with ghost stories set in a mysterious world called Yin. Eventually Olivia travels to China to reconcile her past with the hopes and dreams of her future.

The Bonesetter's Daughter (2001)

This is the story of Ruth Lyui Young and the deterioration of her relationship with her live-in boyfriend Art Kamen. When Ruth's mother is rendered speechless (suffering from Alzheimer's disease), Ruth turns to the diary her grandmother kept as a young woman. Ruth comes to a clearer understanding of her past, her mother's past, and her own difficulties.

The Moon Lady (1992) (a picture book with color illustrations)

Grandmother tells the story (to Maggie, Lily, and June) of her childhood separation from her family and her encounter with the Moon Lady on the night of the Moon Festival. The Moon Lady grants one wish to the young Ying-ying.

Sagwa, the Chinese Siamese Cat (1994) (a picture book with color illustrations)

Ming Miao explains to her five kittens their Chinese (not Siamese) background by telling the story of their ancestor, naughty kitten Sagwa, who lived in the House of the Foolish Magistrate. The Magistrate is known for his foolish rules and his use of cats to print his edicts (he dips their tails in ink). When Sagwa accidentally falls into an inkpot, she blots out one of the words in the Magistrate's newest law. Her mistake causes the Magistrate to become instantly popular with the people and in return he gives all cats a place of honor in his house.

Video and Audio

We have used extensively the DVD of *The Joy Luck Club*, first issued in 1993. Discussions in this book of the film of *The Joy Luck Club* reference this version of the film.

There are many online and printed interviews with Tan, but a particularly interesting one appears on the Academy of Achievement Web site (www.achievement.org/autodoc/page/tan0int-1). The site posts the interview with Tan in written form but also allows viewers to click on Tan's picture and see video and hear audio clips of the interview. Audio (cassette or CD) versions are available for all of Tan's novels and *The Opposite of Fate*. Some are abridged and some include another reader along with Tan.

Resources and Reference Materials

We like the materials available on Web English Teacher (www. webenglishteacher.com). From the homepage, click on Literature/ Prose, then Amy Tan, to access a number of interesting articles (including a Web Quest). These are user-friendly materials that can be downloaded or modified. As mentioned earlier, the Australian Teachers of Media's study guide on the film is noteworthy.

Amy Tan, Harold Bloom's collection of essays in the Modern Critical Views series, is current and useful. He includes a brief introduction and essays by a number of contemporary critics (including the 1995 Salon interview). The book concludes with a chronology of Tan's life and an extensive and up-to-date bibliography.

Amy Tan: A Literary Companion by Mary Ellen Snodgrass, published in 2004, provides analysis of characters and plots in Tan's fiction, along with literary analysis, chronologies of each book, definitions of foreign terms, and writing and research topics.

Chronology of Amy Tan's Life

1952   An-mei Ruth "Amy" Tan born on February 19 in Oakland, California, to John Yueh-han and Daisy (Tu Ching) Tan.

1960   As a third grader at Matanzas Elementary School, Tan publishes "What the Library Means to Me" in the Santa Rosa *Press Democrat*.

1967   Tan loses her brother Peter and, seven months later, her father John, both to a brain tumor. Mother Daisy learns she has a benign tumor and reveals to Tan that she had been previously married in China and had three daughters.

1968   Daisy moves her daughter and surviving son to Switzerland, where Tan enrolls at the Institut Monte Rosa.

1970   Tan enrolls in premed at Linfield, a Baptist college in Oregon, on an American Baptist Scholarship. Meets Louis M. DeMattei, an Italian American law student, on a blind date.

1972   Tan transfers to San José City College and switches from premed to a double major in English and linguistics.

1973   After another transfer, Tan graduates from San José State University with a BA in English. Begins graduate work in linguistics at the University of California at Santa Cruz.

1974   Tan receives an MA from San José State University and marries DeMattei, a tax attorney. Begins doctoral work in linguistics at UC Santa Cruz and later at Berkeley.

1976   Tan leaves graduate school to work in the Alameda County Association for Retarded Citizens, where she works until 1981.

1980   Tan directs MORE, a San Francisco project for children with developmental handicaps.

1981–87 Tan develops successful career as a freelance business writer with clients that include IBM, AT&T, Apple Computer, and Pacific Bell.

1985   Tan begins writing fiction and publishes her first story, "Endgame," in *Seventeen* magazine. Agent approaches her about writing a book outline.

1987   Tan enrolls at the Squaw Valley Community of Writers workshop and begins writing short fiction that is eventually published in magazines, including *Glamour*, *San Francisco Focus*, *Threepenny Review*, and *Grand Street*. In October she travels to China with her mother and meets her half sisters. When she returns in November, literary agent Sandra Dijkstra has six offers for a book contract.

1988   Tan closes her freelance business to become a full-time writer. Completes *The Joy Luck Club* in four months.

1989   *The Joy Luck Club* is published and becomes a bestseller. Receives the Commonwealth Club gold award for fiction, the Bay Area Book Reviewers award for best fiction, and the American Library Association's Best Book for Young Adults award; is nominated for the National Book Critics Circle Award; and is a finalist for the National Book Award.

1990   Tan publishes "The Language of Discretion" and "Mother Tongue."

1991   Tan publishes *The Kitchen God's Wife*, which also becomes a bestseller. Receives honorary Doctor of Humane Letters degree from Dominican College (now Dominican University of California).

1992   Tan publishes *The Moon Lady*, a children's book, illustrated by her friend Gretchen Schields. First sings with a group of fellow authors who become known as The Rock Bottom Remainders, whose proceeds support literacy programs.

1993   Tan writes the screenplay with Ronald Bass for the film of *The Joy Luck Club*, which debuts on Mother's Day.

1994   Tan publishes *Sagwa, the Chinese Siamese Cat*, another children's book, also illustrated by Gretchen Schields.

1995   Tan publishes *The Hundred Secret Senses*, which was short-listed for the Bay Area Book Reviewer's prize. Her mother Daisy diagnosed as suffering from Alzheimer's disease.

1999   Daisy Tan dies on November 22.

2001   Tan publishes *The Bonesetter's Daughter*, which becomes a bestseller. In June she is diagnosed with Lyme disease.

2003   Tan publishes *The Opposite of Fate*, a collection of nonfiction works.

Works Cited

"Amy Tan: Bestselling Novelist." 1996. *Academy of Achievement* Interview (June 18). Aug. 2004 <http://www.achievement.org/autodoc/page/tan0bio-1>.

Bernardinelli, James. 1993. Film review of *The Joy Luck Club*. *Colossus.net*. June 6, 2005 <http://movie-reviews.colossus.net/movies/j/joy_luck.html>.

Bloom, Harold, ed. 2000. *Amy Tan*. Modern Critical Views series. Philadelphia: Chelsea House.

Cao, Lan. 1997. *Monkey Bridge*. New York: Viking Press.

Costanzo, William V. 2004. *Great Films and How to Teach Them*. Urbana, IL: National Council of Teachers of English.

———. 1992. *Reading the Movies: Twelve Great Films on Video and How to Teach Them*. Urbana, IL: National Council of Teachers of English.

Davidson, Hilary. 2003. "Rewriting Fate." *Book Magazine* (Nov.–Dec.): 65–66.

Edwards, Jami. 2004. *bookreporter.com* Interview with Amy Tan (August). June 6, 2005 <http://www.bookreporter.com/authors/au-tan-amy-2.asp>.

Graff, Gerald. 2003. *Clueless in Academe: How Schooling Obscures the Life of the Mind*. New Haven: Yale University Press.

HarperCollins Publishers. 2003. Author Interview: Amy Tan (March). Aug. 2004 <http://www.harpercollins.com.au/authors/author_interview.cfm?Author=0000456>.

Howe, Desson. 1993. Film review of *The Joy Luck Club*. *The Washington*

Post (September 24). June 6, 2005 <http://www.washington post.com/wp-srv/style/longterm/movies/videos/thejoyluck clubrhowe_a0aff7.htm>.

HUNTLEY, E. D. 1998. *Amy Tan: A Critical Companion.* Westport, CT: Green-wood Press.

IVILLAGE. 2004. "Amy Tan: It's All a Learning Experience: An Interview." (August). <http://www.ivillage.com/books/intervu/fict/articles/0,,192468_242700,00.html>.

THE JOY LUCK CLUB. 1993. Dir. Wayne Wang. Screenplay Amy Tan and Ronald Bass. Hollywood Pictures.

KELLY, DAVID. 2003. Critical essay on "Rules of the Game." *Short Stories for Students: Presenting Analysis, Context, and Criticism on Commonly Studied Short Stories.* Vol. 16. Detroit: Gale Group.

LEONG, ANTHONY. 2002. Film review of *The Joy Luck Club. Media Circus.net* (January 24). June 6, 2005 <http://www.embanet.com/entertainment/_disc8/000000cd.htm>.

MACDONALD, JAY. 2003. Interview. "A Date with Fate: Tan's Memoir Probes Cosmic Connections." *BookPage* (November). June 6, 2005 <http://www.bookpage.com/0311bp/amy_tan.html>.

RICO, BARBARA ROCHE, AND SANDRA MANO. 2001. *American Mosaic: Multi-cultural Readings in Context.* 3rd ed. Boston: Houghton Mifflin.

SEE, CAROLYN. 1989. "Drowning in America, Starving for China." *The Los Angeles Times Book Review* (March 12): 1, 11. Aug. 2004 <http://galenet.galegroup.com>.

SNODGRASS, MARY ELLEN. 2004. *Amy Tan: A Literary Companion.* Jefferson, NC: McFarland.

SOMOGYI, BARBARA, AND DAVID STANTON. 1991. "Amy Tan: An Interview." *Poets & Writers Magazine* (Sept.–Oct.): 25–32.

SOURIS, STEPHEN. 1992. "Recent American Multiple Narrator Novels: A Bakhtinian/Iserian Analysis." Diss. University of Wisconsin–Madison.

"THE SPIRIT WITHIN: THE SALON INTERVIEW: AMY TAN." 1995. *Salon.com.* (November 12). Sept. 2004 <http://www.salon.com/12nov1995/feature/tan.html>.

TAN, AMY. 1989. *The Joy Luck Club.* New York: Putnam.

————. 2003. *The Opposite of Fate: A Book of Musings.* New York: Putnam.

TEASLEY, ALAN B., AND ANN WILDER. 1997. *Reel Conversations: Reading Film with Young Adults.* Portsmouth, NH: Heinemann.

TIBBETTS, JOHN. 1994. "A Delicate Balance: An Interview with Wayne Wang about *The Joy Luck Club.*" *Literature and Film Quarterly* 22.1: 2.

WOO, ELAINE. 1989. *Los Angeles Times* (May 12, sec. VI): 1, 14.

XU, BEN. 1994. "Memory and the Ethnic Self: Reading Amy Tan's *The Joy Luck Club.*" *MELUS* 19.4 (Spring): 3–18.

Authors

Renée H. Shea is professor of English at Bowie State University, part of the University System of Maryland and one of the oldest Historically Black Colleges and Universities. Formerly director of English composition, she currently teaches courses in world literature, American autobiography, women's studies, and rhetoric. She is also a member of both the honors and the graduate faculty. Former chair of the NCTE Committee on Comparative and World Literature, she is currently a member of the Commission on Literature. She has worked with the College Board's Advanced Placement English Program for over twenty-five years and coauthored *Teaching Nonfiction in AP English: A Guide to Accompany 50 Essays* (with Lawrence Scanlon). She chairs the Essay Committee for the GED exam and has consulted on assessment issues for school districts and private organizations, including the U.S. Chamber of Commerce. Shea has written extensively on contemporary women writers (including Rita Dove, Edwidge Danticat, Sandra Cisneros, Grace Paley, Julia Alvarez, and Maxine Hong Kingston) in such publications as *Poets & Writers*, *Women in the Arts*, and *Callaloo*. She is the author of two college textbooks, *Essay: Reading with the Writer's Eye* (with Hans Guth) and *A Practical Rhetoric for College Writers* (with Evelyn Taylor).

Deborah L. Wilchek has been a classroom teacher for over thirty years, with teaching experience from kindergarten to adult education and college. Her primary experience as a teacher has been at the high school level. She chaired the English department at Richard Montgomery High School for twenty years and will be implementing a special program at Rockville High School in Rockville, Maryland. She has been an item writer and reviewer for the American Council on Education and has presented at numerous teacher workshops and seminars. Most recently, Wilchek taught creative writing, film studies, peace studies, Theory of Knowledge 1 and 2, and English 11 in the International Baccalaureate Programme at Richard Montgomery High School. She recently wrote a review, "Addition and Subtraction in Oprah Winfrey's *Their Eyes Were Watching God*," published on the AP Central Web site.

■ ■

This book was typeset by Electronic Imaging in Berkeley, Interstate, and Old Style 7.

The typefaces used on the cover include Trebuchet MS and Zurich Ex BT.

The book was printed on 50-lb. Williamsburg Offset paper by Versa Press, Inc.